CHORONZON

VOLUME II
MARTINET PRESS

CHORONZON
VOLUME II
JUNE 2016

ISBN-13: 978-0692723920

ISBN-10: 0692723927

COVER ART by JOEL HRAFNSSON

DISCLAIMER:

All material contained in this document is provided for research and educational purposes only. *Caveat lector*.

TABLE OF CONTENTS

EDITORIAL FOREWORD

This is the second edition of *Choronzon*, and we were very pleased with the sheer number of contributions that the Press received for consideration. Editing a journal of this size is a bit daunting: on the one hand, it's good to give everyone a platform to express their own unique insights into the Abyss. On the other hand, it's mechanically impossible to include everything we receive, and so we've spent hours – literally, hours – going through the emails, photos, PDFs, and docs, trying to see which pieces fit best together. At a certain point, we have had to abandon any kind of professional logic, and just let mad instinct take over. This isn't a question of judgement or assessment – it's rather listening to the whispers at the back of your head, straining to hear the chittering, the tell-tale twitch in your hair, the catch in your breathe when you know (rather: you *know*) that you're looking at a piece that belongs in this collection. All this to say, we're grateful and honored to have a hand in preparing this second edition of *Choronzon*, and we hope that our partners, authors, artists, and readers, are as pleased with the result as we are.

We have received a number of requests for publication, and an increasing number of quality manuscripts. Some of these you will see in 2016, others in 2017. This makes us glad. What does NOT make us glad, though, is the increasing number of people who write us, asking if we can do leather-bound high quality editions like the larger "professional" occult presses. The answer is "yes, we technically *can* – but NO, we're not going to do that." Then, invariable, people write back to say that hardcover makes more money, and they want money, and surely we must want money. And let us be clear: they couldn't be more wrong. We don't do this for money. Period. We want to sell books with good quality editing, that anyone can afford. Anyone who tells you the binding of the book somehow equates to the quality of the content is lying to you, because they want your money. Period. End of story, if you think otherwise, there are about ten other presses that are happy to take your money, or your manuscript.

The moment that a press turns "professional", insofar as they have a fulltime staff, they are commercially dependent on publishing books. That's very dangerous, because it means that the quality of the books is no longer their priority. The quality of their current is no longer their priority. You might feel good by owning their $500 books, and they might genuinely feel good about what they're doing, but let's be clear: you cannot worship the Abyss, and claim to serve it, and still try to make money off people by selling "scripture." If your teacher or guru or shaykh tells you that he wants your money in exchange for books, they are just using you.

Just to be very clear: teachers are important. if your teacher actually gives you real power or teachings or services, that's different – you should *volunteer* your time or sex or money in payment. A real teacher should be shown gratitude – they should not have to *ask* for payment. You should have the sense to give it freely.

But if someone tells you that you should buy expensive books to get their teachings, then that's exploitation. They're not anti-whatever-the-hell they claim to be, they're totally worldly. Tell them to fuck off – seriously, do this – because you don't need that kind of nonsense.

Maybe it would be good to say something further about the spiritual orientation of Martinet Press. We are believers, all of us. We worship the Darkness, without shame or embarrassment. All of us at MP, at some point, have encountered what other people call "dark gods" or "demons" or "djinn". Most people run screaming at that point, but we're not most people. If you're reading *Choronzon*, you're probably like us. You cannot convince people to believe in the Abyss, but you can at least reach out to others who have been touched by It, and help them to express It. This is important, because the Abyss is sacred, and other's experience of It can help you to have greater insights into what the Abyss wants or does not want, and it can help you to find techniques or practices that will OPEN YOU to It, so that it can better invade you, tear you apart, and stitch you back together.

If you asked, 'why are you doing this journal?', we would answer that we recognize that there are many people who serve the spirit world in many ways. The spirit world is real – the Abyss is real. It's not science-fiction. In the 1970s and 1980s, the CIA and KGB both admitted that they had spent years and millions of dollars in trying to understand the hidden mysteries, though neither of them will discuss it today in interviews. The Nazi obsession with the occult is a film trope today. This is not by coincidence: these states understand that occult power is real, it's not simply make believe. If it were entirely make believe, people would not make movies about it. It cannot be reduced to Freudian neurosis and Jungian archetypes. The Darkness is real. Possession happens. There truly are spiritual beings that see humanity as food, and we'd be stupid to ignore all of these facts. If you can get a psychiatrist to speak freely (we have done this), they'll tell you that almost every person in a mental hospital is genuinely ill – but there are sometimes a few cases where someone is genuinely being controlled by an inhuman consciousness, and that terrifies the medical community. This won't be on BBC, but you dig enough in the medical community, and you will see it yourself.

We believe that such powers are real. We have felt them, seen their hands at work. We are committed, body and spirit, to helping bring the next aeon. We don't really care about magic for love or wellbeing. This is about aeonic, cosmic change. Cultures *do* rise and fall. Civilizations crumble. That is because the spiritual powers that feed on humanity do not need one or two sacrifices. They need *wars*, fought in their name, consecrated in their honor. When the Vikings cried before battle '*Jeg gir deg en Odin* (I give you all to Odin)', it was not merely a wish for good luck – it was literally feeding the gods on human lives. What is happening in the east right now – the cultural, national sacrifices of Afghanistan, Iraq, Syria, and Libya – these are not about oil. This is about engineering the new aeon. *Redeunt Saturnia regna* – Saturn's kingdom returns from the Abyss.

This journal is a real grimoire. It provides a ragged map of experiences, insights, visions, and practices through which you can approach the Abyss. Of course, the Abyss is chaos, it has no clear paths, no official churches or orders. But there are traditions, loose enclaves on its shores, which offer a rough kind of shelter to those occultists who have (against all common sense) come seeking the revelations of the void. No one single author can show you the way. But perhaps where one stumbles, many can find the paths together.

Join us, reader. Our names are *legion*.

- Martinet Press

SERGEY KRAMER (DCLXVI)

I

II

III

IV

V

VI

THE AEON OF DARK EMPATHY
Asha'Shedim

When I formed the Lilin Society back in 2013, it was out of disgust and outrage as to what direction the occult arts had devolved, that lead me towards the infernal path I was to pave. My vision was to seek out like minded Satanists (not weekend Satanists) and form a brotherhood where individuals and sects alike could unite and learn under its umbrella. Our goal since the beginning has been simple yet bold. We seek out the path of internal evolution which can be achieved through Pathei-Mathos.

Pathei-Mathos can be defined as an internal process both individual in nature as well as aeonic. It is learning through adversity; it is wisdom gained through personal suffering and personal experience which all lead to gnosis. Gnosis, or hidden knowledge, is discovered through a combination of personal suffering, adversity, the occult arts and personal experiences both internal and external. If one of these is taken away then the practitioner hasn't reached the requirements to evolve toward gnosis. To understand the limits of the clay prison (flesh) and how minuscule we truly are within the cosmos, will bring us closer to gnosis. It will bring about change.

The Lilin Society thus uses techniques such as insight roles and challenging physical tests to fill the requirements of pathei-mathos. Through ritual sorcery, and especially internal sorcery, we truly learn about ourselves, but only with a combination of other techniques. The Lilin Society may provide a tried and tested path toward enlightenment and evolution to those who wish to commit to our standards.

It is the path to gnosis. To slack in one or more areas leads to failure, of delusions of growth, or a false sense of achievement that was not earned. These ignorant beings are unbalanced, absorbed by ego and trade their evolution for an imposter's mask.

With regard to insight roles, there often seems to be confusion as to the purpose they serve. These are roles we willingly take on that purposely place us at odds with ourselves. They are intended to cause inner conflict as well as outer conflict, and thus bring about change and evolution. Becoming a police officer, a right wing fanatic and so forth, are examples of insight roles. I myself have lived the insight role of being the leader of a right wing militia. I supported the Tea Party and took on far right beliefs.

My sudden shift confused the people around me, but the role helped me to gain a greater understanding of myself. Once the insight role had served its purpose, I stepped down as General, and the militia has since disbanded. I have also served in the military as a means to achieve insight. This also served as a form of aeonic sorcery, as I supported the killing force that fought Muslims, a revolting demiurgic cult. These are but a few examples of how I have used insight roles to foster my own personal development. I view insight roles as a key component in one's personal evolutionary path; these roles are important to me as they should be to everyone within the Lilin Society.

As a Society we strive to surpass the mundane and all limitations bestowed upon the mundanes by the cosmic creator. After our limitations are tried and tested by pathei-mathos, we move to learn to kill our ego, and thus free the Azoth. This is done through fasting, self-mutilation, sleep deprivation, psychedelic drug use, and spiritual segregation. Although these tasks are seemingly trivial, they in fact are detrimental to the development of 'Homo Galacticus', a new human which is more concerned with the internal rather than the external world. This willful shaping and molding of the mind makes us more capable of understanding and receiving gnosis.

We all have the ability to evolve, but it is our contentment within a material world that prevents many of us, especially the mundane, from achieving it. It is our material anchors which tether us to this world and deny us the liberation our spirit strives for: to filter back into timeless chaos. We must break the cycle of rebirth and evolve.

Neophytes within the society often ask me where they should begin. The occult arts can be a labyrinth of possibilities that may confuse one as much as it inspires another. My suggestion is to begin with meditation, for it is meditation that is the root of all successful work. Without a mind detached from the body, the wand and altar are simply material objects without any real power or use. It is the clear mind that communicates with the acausal world which empowers the tools and rituals of Satanism.

Satanists must wrap their mind around the concept of the acausal world, one full of acausal spirits liberated of physical form. Satan is one of many acausal spirits that reside in the other side, but he is simply one of many. A typical misconception is that Satan is the supreme god of chaos, this is not true. The Unknown God is ruler of all cosmic chaos and Satan rules the worlds of Sitra Achra as he looks up to the unmanifested womb to return to chaos.

From this acausal world, we have acausal energies which can be used. This is the true basis of sorcery. The Lilin Society posits that every man and every woman is a nexion to the acausal world. How this is so can be observed through life itself, even within the mundane aspects of materiality. Everything in the universe, from a pencil on a desk, to an asteroid in the sky, needs force to move. This is the cause and effect of the causal world, yet we can move without force simply by thinking it. I tell my arm to move and it does. This is evidence of an outside energy at odds with the causal world within us. We are full of acausal energy and thus we all serve as a nexion to the acausal world. Plants have acausal energy and thus this is why herbal sorcery works. To understand the acausal is to understand sorcery.

Acausal empathy, dark empathy, and sinister empathy are all different terminology describing the sensitivity to (and awareness of) acausal energies. It is beyond causal abstractions, beyond all casual symbols, and beyond occultism, for the occult uses causal symbols and methods to access the acausal. It is thinking in acausal time rather than the cause and effect of causal time.

Acausal beings are beyond our understanding. Some of these acausal beings only exist within the realm of the acausal while others have the means to manifest within this world. These are the demons that we may contact or call upon. They are without physical form but can take a causal form within this world. These beings are beyond morality and causal concepts. It is impossible to hold them to our definition of morality. They exist by their own acausal nature. Acausal beings have the ability to feed off of emotion. They also feed off of energy, such as the *prana* in blood during a sacrifice (or bloodletting ritual), during the burning of herbs and incense, and so on. They do not live and die for they are eternal.

The examination of the acausal thus brings me to discuss humanity and the causal. Energy cannot neither be created nor destroyed. Our consciousness is energy. Since it cannot be destroyed, it thus 'lives' forever, surviving the death of the body; it may move toward either the acausal world or may be locked into the vicious cycle of rebirth. Another key word here is created.

The creator god has created our body, created our soul, but our spirit was stolen from this acausal world. It has been imprisoned in this clayform, and in a sense lives in an insight role here in the causal world. This struggle strengthens the spirit as we find gnosis and fight to break the chains of rebirth.

It should also be noted that acausal beings are not restricted by causal travel. Causal travel is physical, and they are not physical beings, and thusly not restricted by the laws of our physical existence. They are all encompassing and everywhere at once. Some are more powerful than others.

While some can bring about change within the causal world others cannot, just as some cannot manifest within the causal world.

Here I would like to discuss Baphomet, as there seems to be some confusion over how she is viewed within the Lilin Society. The Lilin Society stands in agreement with the Order of Nine Angles in that Baphomet is the mother of Earth. She is the blood crazing shapeshifter whom has the ability to enter the causal world. It should be noted that this manifestation of Baphomet has nothing to do with the effigy worshipped by the Templars, although we do use this archetypal image since it is so widely identified as Baphomet.

Satan, Baphomet, and the myriad other demons described above are not gods. They are not to be worshipped, feared or obeyed. They are to be admired and respected at all times, but to worship them goes against the law of a Satanist for a Satanist bows before no man nor god. Usage of terms such as 'Lord' and 'Master' are offered out of respect, but do not have a binding restraint to them. We feed them energy and in exchange they thus bring about the change we ask for.

These demons are often considered 'evil', a term which seems to linger around Satanists as a whole. Now this is true in that these demons are void of morals and thus do not uphold the "laws" of human morality. A Satanist is a reflection of these demons, and thus is also 'evil' in this sense. This 'evilness' digs deeper and manifests itself within us as we further delve into aeonic sorcery and sinister acts. We condone and encourage these actions in order to evolve the spirit and fight causal abstractions.

Causal abstractions may be defined as anything man-made or imposed with the purpose of controlling the populace. Everything from government to demiurgic religions should be viewed as causal abstractions. Laws based on morals rather than honor (and the courts which uphold these laws), forced taxation by a state or nation, the education system and all its manipulation, should all be viewed as systems of mind control. These are all tyrannical forms of the demiurge put into the hands of mankind to impose false order. These abominations must be fought, for in order to fully evolve as a populace, we must shed ourselves of causal abstractions. How can we fight the war of the spiritual when the war of the physical stands in our way?

It should be noted that human sacrifice exists within the Lilin Society, but this is performed in a way to prevent the Satanist from going to prison. In the old days, blood was shed before Baphomet and the killer bathed in the blood. Today we must take a more subtle approach to avoid the lengthy jail terms that would restrict us from evolving. We perform all human sacrifice through sorcery, but that is not to say we do it indiscriminately. The art of culling is just that, an art, and the sacrifice must be chosen as a means to benefit Satanism. This is the first task. One must ask "How does the death of this person affect Satanism?" Then the potential sacrifice is tested, tried and finally selected. Our sacrifices are an art and we always adhere to these methods.

In regard to rituals and ceremony the question is often posed as to whether the practitioner can change or add to what has been written for the Lilin Society. Not only is this fine but it is encouraged and expected in order to make the rituals and ceremonies more personalized, and thus more effective. The rituals, the symbols, the steps and so forth are all causal in nature. They are tools to aid us in tapping into the acausal, but they are just that, tools. If you feel, for example, that a step is unnecessary then you may omit it and perhaps replace it with something you feel is more beneficial to yourself. The only requirement is that all rituals performed must adhere to the rules of the Lilin Society in order for them to be used within the umbrella of it's name. This is not to say that you may not go beyond the rules (for as we say, rules are causal in nature) but if you choose to do so they are considered solitary rituals which are not to be conducted under our name.

I have received a litany of criticism since the Lilin Society was formed. It seems that many feel that it doesn't need to exist, for Satanism is a solitary path. This is true, but since causal abstractions exist and imposed order exists, and we operate in a causal world, I ask then, what is wrong with uniting like-minded, elite, evolved beings who all wish to learn together and evolve? This antisocial behavior is a product of misanthropy which is a characteristic of the Satanist and although there is nothing wrong with this ideology of hatred, there is also nothing wrong with uniting and working together.

I would like to conclude this essay with a description of the Order of the Dreccs. The Order of the Dreccs is a sub-group built within the Lilin Society. These are individuals devoted to the Laws of the Sinister-Numen. The Sinister-Numen are those who represent types of acausal energy within the causal world. They are sorcerers that have the ability to inspire and influence even the mundanes.

Through the Laws of the Sinister-Numen they spread aeonic sorcery to aid in the collapse and overthrowing of any and all causal abstractions. They are a danger to the system, for they are as charismatic as they are dangerous.

The Dreccs blend into society, and purposefully so. They are cops, lawyers, doctors, cashiers, mechanics, etc. Some take insight roles and become political or even religious figures. They appear to contribute to societal order, but it is only a mask that they wear for their true goals are to decimate all causal abstractions. The Dreccs are dissidents willing to fight this Earthly battle through physical action, deception and aeonic sorcery.

The path of the Drecc is a solitary path, even more so than that of a typical Satanist. Dreccs do not know about one another. Many people don't even know that they are Satanists, but just exist as such.

There are no Drecc meetings or get-togethers. The Drecc is a Lilin Society member, but within the Lilin Society their Drecc status is a secret.

A good example of a Drecc engaging in an insight role is to become a catholic priest. To the community the deception is real and from within the church he will cause havoc and chaos. When the chaos comes to fruition, no one will suspect the Drecc, for he is a good actor and plays his part well. If the Drecc's insight role involves him marrying a mundane to keep the role going, he will not fall in love with her. He will in secret raise his children to be Satanists and once the role is over he will divorce his mundane wife. Not everyone is cut out to be a member of the Lilin Society, and not every member is cut out to be a Drecc. Only the elite among the elite will live this lifestyle, and the reward of spreading the sinister will be well deserved.

LAURENT BRAUN

HADOWDANCE

SOMBRE EVEIL I

SOMBRE EVEIL IV

BEHOLDER OF THE EYE
Orlog Volksgeist

PART I: THE POLEMIC

I will explain precisely what this article is from the start: a forthright attack on all things containing racism, racialism or segregationalist approaches to Reconstructionist Heathenism, Germanic Neo/Paleopaganism as well as any and all attempts to resurge the atavism of the Northern past. While the concurrent scene is largely affected by the disease known as contemporary xenophobia, along with the insecurities instilled upon a largely underdeveloped body of people who lack an entire millennium of consciousness, it serves to remember that at the end of the day, those Heathens that rescind the progressive time-span of human evolution (up to and including the complete rejection of the development of pluralist, polyglot and metropolitan areas) are actually the lessers in terms of aeonic pursuits.

From a purely selfish standpoint, the individual is oftentimes much more distinguished amidst a societal subgroup when their unique philosophy of living is patented and crafted by experience, and not books alone. This means that even in a European thoroughbred scenario, the proper execution of an esoteric *anados* would be largely populated with unique differentiation. Alas, this is still yet not a case even within a scenario as limited as this. It seems that the bane of Heathenry is that it is entirely stuck upon a loose and often contorted apprehension of historic and skaldic writ.

Special interest groups would have you believe that the Vikings of ancient Europe, and the expanding Germanic tribes lived in a glorious, hyper-moral and "racialist" manner; such an understanding is immolated upon even the barest contact with documented, unchanged and well-researched anthropological study. The Vikings, the Germanic Tribes and the indigenous people of Central and Northern Europe existed in a time of hard conditions.

Such conditions included: War, Famine, Disease and a brutal, unforgiving climate. These banes alone, if applied to a modern society would find that their inclinations towards bigotry were dashed upon jagged rock- at least for those units of people who are evolved enough to understand the value of social politics, cooperation and "actual" folkish ethos, opposed to using it simply as a front-word for racism.

Vikings, Germanic Tribes and the indigenous people of Central and Northern Europe had very little diction concerning who, how and what manner of philosophy could or should relate to their spouses and tradition of loving. Considering the nature of war in the middle ages, it was not uncommon for a band of Viking retainers, a Germanic Tribe or a collection of people from Central or Northern Europe to gather the women of a defeated enemy, targeted encampment, village or country. Therefore, it would not be uncommon to find, in the actual historical scenario that occurred, a Spanish, an Etruscan or even a Semitic line or many such various lines existing and intermingling within the ancient past of Scandinavia. The supposition could go on from here, but I will leave that to open-ended follow-ups that vector into the interested parties.

There is a long standing misconception of the genetic makeup of these peoples, oftentimes propagated by sundry sectors of the media, seeking to capitalize on basal and mundane perceptions. Too many mediums of the surrounding nature incorrectly conclude that the Nordic, based on a fantastical and visionary advancement alone, were entirely tall, blonde-haired and blue-eyed clones of one another. Due to the above posited facts, this is known widely, among the academics of the field, to be a blatant and childish falsity. Though, an error that even you believe while also knowing it to be as such is the deadliest of inaccuracies, because there is an ulterior motive and it was orchestrated by some divisional, divergent and mentally detrimental agency.

There is an old Saxon word known as "*beblonden*." A verb as it is, used then to denote the process of dying one's hair blonde, because it was seen as ideal. Here is crucially important the weltanschauung of the Germanic mind: in matters of aesthetics, personal relations, love and war. Being that the Sagas of the Icelanders describe a pre-political living scenario not dissimilar to socialism and perhaps in some black and baleful vision of communism, the idea of uniformity, albeit predating standardized dress format, was ideal for the people of the time. The factors which lent to individuality were seen as unsavory, as collectivism was a defense mechanism that allowed humanity to not just survive, but flourish in the pre-Christian and early transitional eras. Nearly all forms of disputes happened to be settled via dueling with swords. All of these conflicts were driven by the power of someone opposing a community effort of the folk.

The Aesir, of which were fabled to have come from Asia (through Turkey and yet even deeper still), would have naturally been, if truly human -or of some acausal hybridization- possessing of darker, even Black contours of hair, with brown eyes as a commonality. The Vanir however were the indigenous deities of the Northern European geographical area, and by these standards they would have been mythically and imaginatively contrasted against the swarthy, gruff barbarian brunettes of the East, leaving a paler and blonder, perhaps even an altogether "lighter" archetype altogether. Freyja, being the mythic Goddess of (among many other things) Love, and the matters of such, would if no other situation allowed for it to be stated directly – be blonde-haired. Therefore, a woman dying her hair using the elements might have been attempting to attune herself visually with the features of the acausal patron of love and lovers. In war, it was a common technique in Scandinavians to contrast their enemies in

appearance, and since the majority of the world is brunette, a Germanic berzerker would clothe himself in everything imaginable that would seem "inhuman" to a foreign brigade. This would include everything from the lycanthropic practices of therianthropy, the donning of bear (*berzerker*) and wolf (*ulfhednar*) skins, consuming mind altering vegetations, painting their bodies with mud, blood, everything in-between, and finally dying their hair, to appear, for lack of any better term in the English language, to be demons and not men.

The only purveyors of the racial element in modern Reconstructionist Heathenism, Germanic Neo/Paleopaganism as well as any and all attempts to resurge the atavism of the Northern past, are those individuals entirely bereft of the Viking spirit of conquest, those lacking the lust for adventure and experience of new and unchartered things. They are those people who are entirely unlike the figure of WOTAN, who, in many legendary tales, oftentimes endured humiliation for experimenting with things that were considered "taboo" or "off limits." It is they who run contrary to the Dark Wotanic Heathen current of ever-seeking knowledge, gnosis and the nector of understanding.

PART II: DRAUGR'S DRAUMAR

It was a hot summer night in New Jersey, filled with nothing but the longstanding turmoil of what has been elsewhere stated as, "The Dark Night of the Soul." Without brandy (my preferred drink at the time), to quell my heavy thoughts, and with the sadness of what had been sacrificed on the Altars of Hel, I lay awake and still in a twin sized bed, with nothing but the silence of the night as my companion.

What the hell have I done to myself- I'm sure I asked, thinking of the outlandish and terrible nature of the National Socialist underground scene of which I had longed so eagerly to penetrate, rise ranks in and move, what I had thought at the time, my firebranded spirit into the mess of it all.

Surely I had developed. My eyes were empty and saw past the automobiles and modern gadgets (at the time, cellular phones were barely a thing- if you had one they were poorly comparable to the handheld computing devices we have today). I was unimpressed with computers of any kind, video games and all the fetishes of my peer groups, save for the art of cinema and music – and yet these mediums were just a repurposed ancient traditions ripped through time.

When I thought of home, I would think of a cottage in a forestral settling, with a single other inhabitant, being HER, with perhaps a few animals – cats of course, and a snake maybe. Though, just the two of us was fine, far removed from the political trites of today, yesterday and tomorrow.

I reached out and captured the moment given when I saw the runes of what I had actually loved of it all- the adventure, the carnage and the tales to be told in the aftermath. Though now I saw what I wanted most – solitude and companion-ship. This all in my waking thoughts, and when I closed my eyes I saw HIM.

Robed in the shades of night, and with a wide brimmed hat, he advanced towards me with a grim and foreboding countenance. He held a long, cruel, and pale finger towards me as if gesturing to identify his purpose of arrival, and then the shadow voice effluviated from his mouth like the collective scream from a murder of ravens.

Though neither in English nor in German, the only two languages I had commanded at the time, I understood his words which were not words, but a truth that came from more than just this figure's mental computation, but from somewhere beyond in some long lost and forgotten saga.

And I understood. The next morning I called my gang leader up on his landline: a number restricted for emergencies, and announced my departure from the movement. I wanted to learn and discover the truth about my past, so that the fire inside would forever last.

DUAN MORATHI
A.A.Morain

Hidden amidst a thicket of dense pine trees and rotted fences, at the end of an old and forgotten dirt road, sat a dilapidated cottage. It was built with stone, now covered in moss and dead ivy, which snaked up its walls and encircled the grubby windows- windows which were cluttered with various items which obscured an outside view. Those windows which did allow such a view were blacked out with large dark sheets, stained and greyed with age.

In this shadowed and rotting cottage, an old woman was sat. The furniture – a haphazard collection of makeshift design and worn with age – were pushed into every corner, allowing for maximum space in the centre of the main room. Every corner, save for one. This corner had been decorated with bizarre and harsh looking symbols, and black lines had been drawn along the wall and the floor, so as to give the impression of an extra set of dimensions or angles.

She lived alone, her young niece and apprentice having long left on her 21st year, to go out into the world and continue the work they had both been born into. She was out there, somewhere, fulfilling the dark task of guiding the coven; of presencing the Dark.

The old crone sat with various items around her, not least of which was a large brazier which dispensed a gratuitous amount of thick smelling incense into the room. Candles were her only light, as she read from an old, mouldy tome, muttering to herself as she did so.

She picked up a large piece of quartz, carved into the shape of a tetrahedron, wiped her blood upon it, and began a guttural and alien chant.

The woman begins to sway, as the atmosphere becomes charged and the corners of the room grow darker. She continues in her reverie for some time, the chant becoming more pronounced and her movements becoming altogether more trance like.

She looks toward the corner where she has facilitated a doorway – a doorway through which They and she will pass following the culmination of the rite.

She feels energy drawn from the crystal, tingling her hands. The crystal – which had been buried with her dead partner for some time now, before her unearthing it and which had been used since then in rather horrific rituals, rituals which involved the termination of life of three worthy opfers- was to be the key to the gate. She knew this much.

The corner grew darker as the air grew thicker, and in her trance the old woman saw a familiar figure step through a rent, twisted in an obscene shape and fashion, the likes of which were common only to the strange and chthonic world this entity inhabited.

The old crone clasped a murky goblet in her hand, keeping the crystal in the other, and drank the contents till there was nothing left.

With that, she convulsed, retching into death under the watchful gaze of the dark visitor.

Death came swiftly, thanks to the expert blend of herbs gathered for this very rite. The old woman stepped toward the doorway, now free of her mortal flesh, and became one with the shadows. She was now a shade, a hag, a veritable Lich. Her life's work now complete, she would haunt the night, and infest the dreams of mankind. Her face would become the face of nightmares for all time.

Together she and He passed through into the shadows, where she would be privy to the blackest of power. The house was left empty, an

old woman's corpse left in a dark cottage
nestled deep in the moors of Yorkshire.

ERICA FREVEL

FEEDS ON THE CHILDREN

PUNISHMENT

RISE OF THE WOLF'S BLOOD

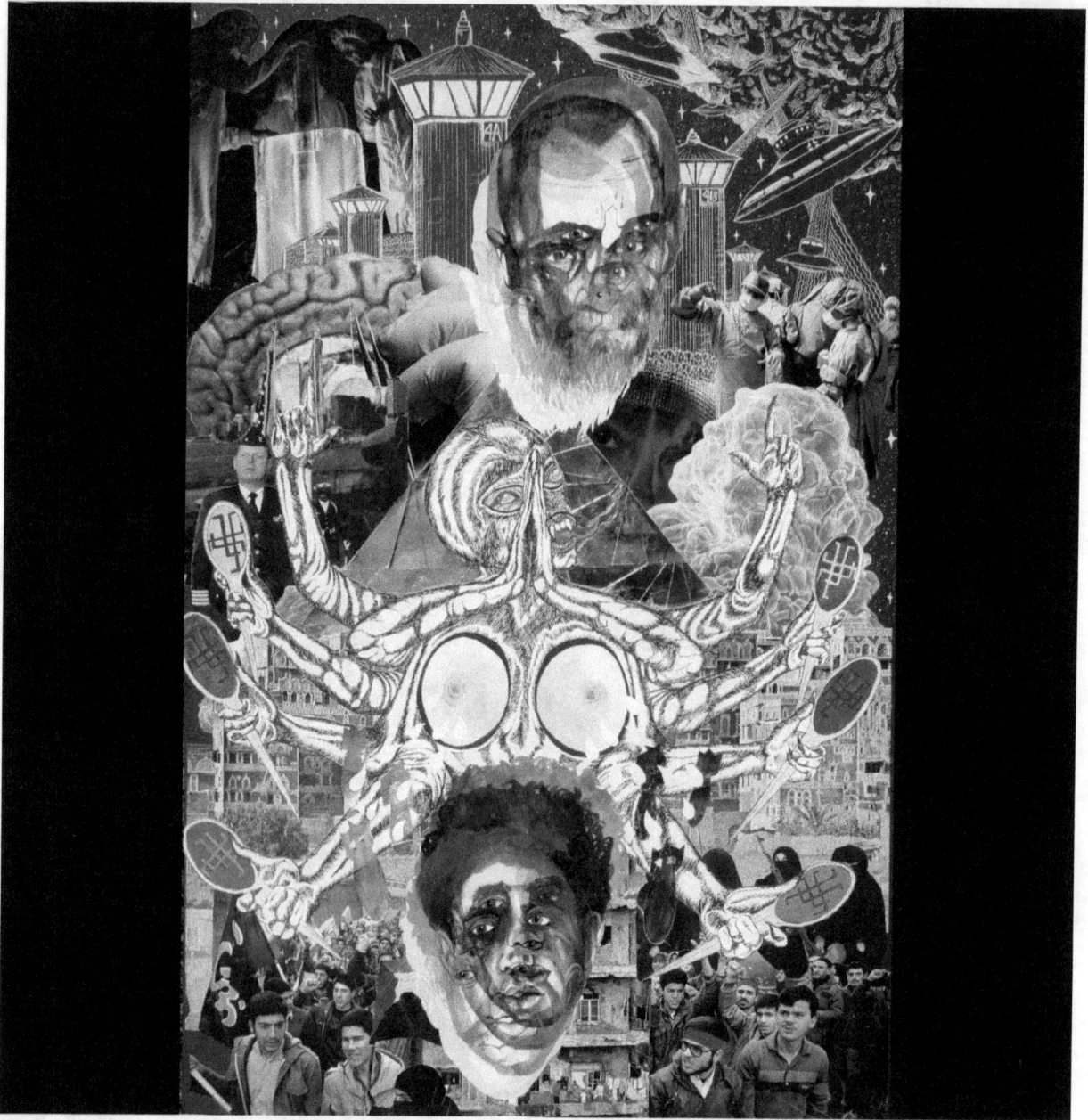

SATANIC SHRAPNEL

THE LION'S PAW
Shadow

With the current mists surrounding African Diasporic Traditions and charlatan imposters capitalizing on interested parties with no knowledge of them, I feel it appropriate that a manuscript be set forth to make visible some of the gates of such paths for sincere seekers who may genuinely be called to them. In composing this article I collaborated directly with personal friends of mine who grew up in these cults in both the US and the Caribbean. In their own words one mist know the value of the source and not the unwanted fans and watered down spin-offs. These things indeed belong first and foremost to their own cultural context.

Anyone in western society who has explored world spiritual traditions in any degree has inevitably crossed someone or another peddling the so-called "dark secrets of voodoo". This is about as absurd as attempting to sell Christianity here in the west as being "dark" and "secretive". In Haiti, Vodou is viewed in a benevolent light-hence the terminology employed by priests and priestesses such as "Bon Hougan" or "Bon Manbo", meaning "Good Priest/ess". Essentially the same as a practitioner of magick identifying them self as a "good witch" or "white witch". Vodou is called *Ginea* or *Fran Ginén* which means it is actually viewed as a Right Hand Path and an open mainstream religion which anyone may initiate into. In the Southern US as well, Voodoo enjoys a sinister reputation but in reality is merely a watered down version of Haiti's religion and in many cases even mixed with Yoruba Orisha traditions becoming even more deluded and ineffective. When people whisper of reanimation of corpses, werewolves in the countryside, or serpents appearing from the corners of the room defying explanation by modern science, they are not speaking of Vodou. These things are hints of heavy black magick which has been hidden in the forests of Haiti for centuries. Many westerners have initiated into Vodou in futile attempts to learn dark secrets, and simply became monetary pawns for Vodoun Temples in Haiti's safer suburbs to bring in money, but further into the green mountainous regions of the island, isolated from the world in a peculiar way where westerners are not readily welcome, there is a secret society hidden beyond the open peristyles of Vodou.

The true horrors which own the night in Haiti belong to a more obscure and little known tradition called *Makaya*, or in some cases *Sect Rouj* meaning "Red Sect" due to the distinct crimson clothing worn at the rites and ceremonies, as well as their association with blood and fiery energies. Unlike Vodou, Makaya is not a religion. It is pure magick, unrestricted by religious doctrine or superstition of consequence for evil, and it was *designed* by both the rite's founders as well as the spirits *moving through them* to act as a point of intrusion for the Dark into this world. This is the form of sorcery employed by the *Bizango* and *Sanpwel*-secret societies on the island spoken of as 'Sacred Police' by the Vodoun Priesthood, but only out of fear as in reality they function more along the lines of Spiritual Terror Squads in rural communities. Makaya is feared because it is highly aggressive sorcery renowned for its power in malefic workings and steeped with rumors of altars with children's coffins, physical shapeshifting, zombification for enslavement, and even human torture to appease cruel and feral entities which feed on such energy. It is an entirely separate tradition with its own initiation rites and unlike the open religious services of Vodou it is a very closed off community. Initiates have passphrases and gestures to identify one another from different houses in much the same manner as Freemasonry. The word *Bokor* actually means "worker" and never had anything to do with Vodou, but was a reference to a worker of Makaya just as *Sevituer* or "servant" signified a practitioner of Vodou.

While there are certainly interesting and provenly effective new developments such as the work of Michael Bertiauxe and David Beth which approach the currents of Vodou in an unconventional manner (perhaps even expanding upon previously unexplored potential in theurgy), there are also many groups and developments claiming direct authenticity which are not at all. Nowadays the exploring student must sift through insulting volumes of westernized trash claiming to be "authentic left hand path voodoo" from mythical "butterfly" cults. There is no such thing, period. To quote the late Prince Nicholas de Vere, "*Real magic is at work here. A group of secretly initiated individuals are turning dross into gold. Fools give charlatans good money in exchange for utterly useless garbage. Now that's alchemy!*" Many Hougans and Manbos (Priests and Priestesses) online will claim such for business but Vodou is in fact referred to as 'working with the right hand' and *Makaya* is working with the Left. Those claiming to be *Sevi Demen* or "work with both hands" are either Hougans with only hear-say knowledge in Makaya because they are uninitiated or Bokors using the title of Hougan as a mask for their darker practices. Initiation into Bizango/Makaya opens a door that can never be closed. Like Quimbanda the forces channeled are fiery, hot, sometimes maddening energies and one simply does not have the option of ever returning to the life they knew once the spirits 'take your head'. A permanent cohabitation will be sealed.

Unlike Vodou which has its roots in Benin/Dahomey, Makaya finds its origins in the rainforests of the Congo, as well as the island of Haiti itsself where the African slaves first made contact with the feral spirits dwelling in local caves and forests. The word "Makaya" is found in several dialects of Bantu/Ki-Kongo language and translates as "leaves" or "sorcery". Like Palo Mayombe there are even remnants of the feared *Anyoto* Cult known to most as the Leopard Men- hints of the shapeshifting practices of the Sanpwel Soldiers which patrol the forests of the island by night. The term *Sanpwel* literally translates as "Hairless Pigs". The Rite was formed by subversive insurgents during the revolution in Haiti, thus their observances are aggressive, militant and dangerous to happen upon, unlike the "*fet*" parties "in honor of God and the spirits" in Vodou. The spirits served include a vast spectrum of *Djab* (demonic entities) and *Lwa* (spirits) whose names and *veves* (sigils) are generally not spoken of outside private counsel or ceremonies. Many of them cannot be served uninitiated and some must be passed or "introduced" to an initiate by his or her mentors directly. Similar to Vodou, Makaya does teach that among the many Lwa and Djab there is one spirit called the *Met Tet* ("Master" or "Mistress of the Head") which acts as not merely a "Patron" but a sort of Mother or Father to the practitioner and it is believed that to understand this entity is to gain a deeper understanding of one's self. This concept is largely shared within African Diasporic Traditions, and for good reason. When I worked security at a nightclub I used to watch intoxicated men and women swoon into threshold states as fast paced rhythms thundered in the atmosphere and hypnotic laser lighting distorted their vision, shy women suddenly stomping and spinning in an almost violent display of power and even straight men jerking and contorting into intensely erotic feminine dancing. With what I learned in these specific systems I could immediately identify such deviations from their societal personas as not just their shadow selves surfacing, but in fact reflections of their spirit guides, bleeding through because they were in a receptive and dissociative state. This is the same method employed in ceremonial dance where the spirits 'mount' or 'ride' a dancer in full possession. In Brazilian Quimbanda for example, it is taught that one's personality is modeled according to energetic impulses emanated from one's Crown *Exu* and *Pomba Gira*, and to explore those impulses is one aspect of worship which leads toward a personal gnosis of one's self and the secrets of one's Exus and their powers. I realized that the same technique may also be applied in exploring one's deviant or abstract impulses in Makaya as an approach to mapping a personal understanding of one's Met Tet and further unlocking one's own shadow-self. A friend and spiritual sister initiated in Makaya when asked about this told me "The Lwa that walk with you have been watching you since you were a child, they knew you long before you knew them. Your Met Tet was actually passed to you by an ancestor. If you choose to walk this path they will teach *you* about who *you are*." In the same sense of acting as a guardian to their children, once 'seated' in the initiated vessel, if for example a vampire were to approach one in the astral, they would be intentionally allowed to take in ones energy, only to suffer the brutal effects thereof at the hand of the initiate's Met Tet.

What is key with this unique stream of divinity is that like the private and true cult of La Catrina (Santa Muerte) the keepers of these paths must approach you, one cannot petition entrance. I have had to discover what practices I simply have no place in and other doors which were opened to me for a reason. As the saying goes concerning *Kafou* Himself in relation to not only the cemetery but all roads; "*If the Master does not give, the Gates will not receive.*" Often they will visit in dreams or will send their devotees into your life to cross paths with. Sometimes when one undertakes *Konzo* (initiation into Vodou) a spirit will demand that they initiate into Makaya as well if it is in their Dharma to do so. More aggressive and predatory *Gadés* ("guards"-protective spirits which act like attack dogs) will be received, and the 'worker' will be assessed on how far they should go through the initiatory levels. Those who initiate into Makaya contrast it brilliantly to initiation in Vodou, stating it is far more electrifying and intense. Baron Kriminel is often one of the first to take interest in one being called, as a hint for those contemplating…For those who feel called to walk with Djab in this life and if the Djab and Lwa grant them passage, I hope this article may be of use in your becoming.

Madame Lisifi vire je m' wouj

- **Shadow**

LERA'S TORMENT
Aubrey Wood Basnight

PART 4

It was all but a blur between the scene at the intersection and finding himself sitting in the designated location – a small cafe – he seated in the al fresca seating outside as per directions which had been previously relayed before the assigned meet, the small iron-wrought chairs around a similarly iron-wrought dining table, simple yet tasteful cloth upon which sat a carafe of water, covered awning above blocking as best it could the glare of the desert sun – already bright and dangerous by midmorning.

He was predictably early despite his brief interlude prior in transit – a habitual earliness which had ground itself into force of habit and behaviour since his youngest years and which had only become more pronounced as time and his paranoia continued to blossom into full flower, the seeds of which however had been long implanted.

Max hoped in this case that he had been the first to arrive, before the dealer – allowing him sometime to rest himself if only briefly and to gain a sense of his immediate surroundings as he slumped graciously into the proffered chair and accepted the small glass of the extra-potent coffee which was indigenous to the area.

There were few non-locals in this part of the city, though he did spot a rather posh couple through the window panes which displayed some small portion of the interior of the cafe, despite the glare. Both of them blondes, both with longish hair including the man, the woman with a shock of black dyed on the sides from the roots to the tips. Strange. But then again, the area – this area especially – tended to attract unusual souls – himself included. The man spotted him as he was offered his seat by the waiter, only a brief glance then a look of unmistakable upper-class disdain and disapproval before returning to a muted conversation with his much more attractive feminine counterpart. Business partners? Lovers perhaps? Anthropologists in repose? Max neither had the time nor energy to speculate overmuch as, glancing at his watch, he noted that the time of his scheduled meeting was almost immediately upon him. His host could, in fact, be sitting in the cafe even now – casing him out from some meticulously obscure booth – head peeping out from behind a newspaper. Perhaps wearing a disguise of some sort, or perhaps he had been disguised during their meeting in North America months before – in order to keep his genuine features unidentifiable by his client who was still at that time undergoing preliminary vetting.

That he had made it this far however indicated to Max that he had been vetted to satisfaction during the interim between then and now – elsewise a decidedly nefarious set-up was at play – for to carry the amount of currency that Max had upon his physical person, in this location of all locations, was foolhardy at best. His contact had insisted beforehand however – no lockers, no travellers' cheques , no discreet wire transfers through a friendly foreign bank – currency ready on hand in cold harsh cash upfront and at the time of the meet, without exception. Max could only but oblige.

The waiter returned to the side of Max's table once again, bringing with him a fresh beverage and an English-language newspaper, which looked to be several weeks old. The man bowed politely and then left with a sharp and practiced turn of the heel, his waiter's tray filled with various beverages and myriad food items balanced precariously high on his left shoulder.

Max sipped the coffee and opened the

newspaper at the exact juncture where the small yellow piece of paper jutted out from between its pages somewhat conspicuously. The two blondes inside the cafe, noticing that Max had opened the paper and received the message, nodded silently to each other and withdrew through the back entrance, unbeknownst to Max himself.

The memorandum contained a second address, only a few blocks away. Leaving a few coins on the table, Max hailed a rickshaw driver, handed him the yellow paper and he was on his way.

PART 5

The rickshaw driver stopped some fifteen minutes later before what appeared to be a large warehouse type structure, all rusted corrugated metal sticking out from here and there, gigantic padlocks on several enormous bay entrances and barred windows set so high above the level of the street that not even the most ambitious of thieves would be able to manage entrance.

Max was not sure at first that he had reached the correct location but after some brief words with the rickshaw driver and pointing at the address on the paper his hired ride was insistent that this was indeed the specified destination. He thanked the man, tipped him generously and then disembarked shakily from the contraption. The driver gave him a particular wide and toothy grin, before pedaling off into the mob, raising one hand behind him to wave a farewell.

Max approached the service door to one side of the building's front, designed specifically for human-size entry and exit in contradistinction to the bay entrances and bearing beside it a small metal protrusion fitted with a battered callbox, one black button for transmission and one red button designed for the buzzer alone. Max pressed for the buzzer and waited, no sound from within penetrating through the thick steel entrance. After several seconds he heard the sound of the door being unlocked from inside by an automatic remote electronic mechanism.

He stepped into the relative darkness, the contrast between standing under the bright unclouded sun taking him several seconds more after stepping through to allow his eyes to adjust before closing the door behind him.

The former factory and/or warehouse – he could not readily ascertain by the contents he could glimpse and the dullness of the lighting – seemed to be long derelict. There was no visible machinery and the high-hung windows along the width and breadth of the building only served to let in a decidedly pale and somewhat funerary light, the solar rays being generously filtered through decades of collected grime.

In the distance he could see a small area in the middle of the building that had been converted into a small open-air sitting room – a few chairs and settees set out on an old crumbling rug – a table – a few antique lamps plugged into a circuit breaker attached to an orange extension cord which made a crazy trail beyond the strange little area, off into the darkness of another sector of the structure.

The sitting area, however, was inhabited – to his relief, he saw, by the contact he had met before in North America. The dealer. Better the devil he knew than the devil he didn't in this case, so he mused to himself.

"Max!" the man called, affectatiously robust, standing and gesturing him forward.

Having crossed the brief distance and sitting down now across from each other over the table, the shortish man poured a small quantity of good single malt from a corked bottle, apologizing unnecessarily to his client that he had no ice available at the moment. Max would have preferred bourbon, but no mind. The alcohol helped to counteract the long morning in slum – sloughing away the fatigue of his recent flight and the subsequent jet lag – and coalescing the scene of the fell princess and the procession he had witnessed early into the morning within his mind in a framework which felt pleasurable rather than one that filled him with dread, as he had experienced in the immediate aftermath during the walk to the cafe. The potential intelligence officers – the fracas at the mouthway of the thoroughfare – all forgotten for the time being, as a sense of mania built within him knowing that the object of his desire was literally within a few square feet in proximity to his person.

The dealer had not even considered bringing the item to North America during discussions held in initial meetings, much to Max's immediate displeasure at the time. Too dangerous, the smallish man had stated emphatically. Too risky, he had underlined with a shaking of his head, waggling of his fingers, small beady eyes beneath raised eyebrows. What then, Max had argued at the time, about the risk to him? About him having to bring it out of a country with a less than favorable rating in the CIA's worldbook – perhaps requiring a mandatory cursory screening by U.S. Homeland Security personnel on his way back into his country of residence? The dealer smiled with false apology and stretched his hands out in a gesture of expansive and patently false regret. Simply not possible, he had said. Simply not possible. The item would not, could not be let out of the country until proper arrangements had been made. There were security concerns on all side, the dealer had soothed, but he was simply the middleman, he could only arrange insofar as the owners of the precious and rare item were willing to accommodate.

The single malt was imbibed by both parties, the reminisces fading under the nigh instantaneous effect of the alcohol, the dealer grinning in a predatory fashion while Max smiled reciprocally, nervously but somewhat like a madman, his mania growing by the minute. The dealer knew that he was purposefully toying with Max – the exchanged pleasantries and stalling being a mechanism entirely unneeded in what for all effective purposes seemed to be a very clandestine location for their meeting and business at hand, a world away from the relative visibility and public venue in which Max

thought that the transaction would take place initially – prior to receiving the note. He knew that now, at this juncture and whilst in his present location he could easily be mugged – murdered – or worse – with no witnesses and none the wiser.

But would he have been drawn all this way, all the way across the Atlantic, to another continent, a dangerous country, by a man who could have easily defrauded him back in the states with little trouble? He had ready cash at the time and – properly drawn out – he would have fronted the money to the wily North African with only a little persuasion. His commitment to obtaining the specified item was beyond doubt. He had sought it for years now, inquiring in every sordid back-alley from Colombo to Phnom Phnem and this had been his first solid lead in all that time. Yes, he would have given the money over after fifteen minutes of persuasive talk from his contact – easily – with only a promissory of delivery – such was the nature of the obsessed.

Max had not proffered such an arrangement however and the dealer had not asked during their previous meet – but instead insisted upon him travelling to the place of the amulet's current residence and Max, with a sinking feeling in his guts but with an elation beyond all possible elation, had agreed readily. Now, at final long last, the moment of initial realization was upon him.

The dealer lifted a finger – not the finger of a laborer nor a mercenary – but the finger of one imbued with the discernment of objects of antiquity – the finger of a high-tier academician with ample experience in the field, someone who knew his ruins, someone who had held, caressed and perhaps translated on long seemingly endless nights in lone corners of esteemed libraries ancient tomes carrying the most nefarious reputations from the dark past and available for perusal only to the most learned and the most intrepid of scholars.

Ah, here it comes.

PART 6

The dealer nodded his head – rising from his chair but gesturing for Max to retain his seat as he moved into the shadows beyond the light of the small area of lighted space. A minute or two passed and Max found the sweat upon his face and body turning cold, his skin pale and chill in premeditation of the revelation for which he had struggled for so arduously thus far, now finding himself on the cusp of breakthrough at long last. Though the moment would be in a way a completion in and of itself it was in reality only the first leg of his journey.

The dealer returned, holding a small but thick box – like a small crate – with metal rings for carrying. Reoccupying his seat, the man bent down and unlatched the opening of the box, bringing the object out and setting it down on the table directly under Max's line of sight.

The object was about the size of a grenade and picking it up to Max's wonder the weight was almost comparable – anomalous as that was considering that the object was mostly glass, though thickly gilded on all sides but one with what seemed to be very old and very heavy antique pewter, though that alone would have not attributed to the weight density – said weight in comparison to the object itself which would most certainly be a cause of alarm for anyone handling it who was not aware of its unique esoteric properties.

Max raised the orb aloft, positioning it slightly in front of the reddish shade of one of the dim electric lamps on the table, resting his elbow upon the table's surface as he examined it further. The orb was filled with a visibly thick yellowish liquid possessing a high level of viscosity – the appearance of which and context of its presence inside the object itself reminded Max of prai oil, sometimes called "corpse oil" – the ghostly substance used in Thai amulets for the inhabitation of demonic entities, the spirits of children tortured at birth, the undead, the disembodied souls of evil witches and other sundry unsavory preternatural beings favored by the most black-hearted practitioners of animism.

The dealer demonstrated to him how the object was to be used. "Lera's Torment" he stated with a faintly disturbed smile at the corner of his mouth, speaking the name by which it has been known colloquially down throughout the years – its namesake based not on the residing entity within, however, but after its first owner – though 'caretaker' may be the terminology more appropriate.

Despite its circular shape, if the torment was sat down with the glass window set facing upward four small prongs would descend discreetly from the opposite side, securing it upright for the user. One drop of blood, warned the dealer, one drop of blood only and the entity would come. No more. Max did not deign it appropriate to interrogate him further on this point, at the present particular crossroad, though the information was certainly filed for further consideration later on. Seeming to read his thoughts, the dealer looked at him squarely in the eye and indicated without saying a word that propitiation above and beyond the strictured limits which had been specified would be to invite almost certain catastrophe.

Might we test it here, before completing the transaction? Max had inquired. The dealer was aghast. Certainly not, absolutely not, never here, not in my presence. Max was somewhat surprised by the vehemence of the dealer's refusal yet there was little he could do, the dealer still holding all of the cards. Though, if push came to shove, should the dealer suddenly decide to decline to make the sale, Max was fully willing to procure the torment by force despite whatever potential risks and dangers – said risks and dangers which could potentially be very considerable indeed, from associates of the dealer hidden in the darkness of the warehouse to whomever may be waiting back on the street. He had come too far to leave empty handed. And now that he had seen the torment for himself his obsession was complete

– all he wanted to do is put his cash squarely on the table and return to his hotel as quickly as possible and then, wait for the evening.

Again, seeming to read his mind and in lieu of his refusal of Max's suggestion of immediate experimentation, the dealer warned him emphatically that he should not under any circumstances attempt to utilize the torment while still in the country. Max began to protest however the dealer raised his hand to silence him before continuing. Yes, the dealer acquiesced, once the torment was out of his hands there was little he could do – after the exchange it would be in Max's hands to do with as he saw fit. However, the dealer began (and here, the caveat, Max predicted) – while this was the case, Max was still in his country. He tapped the desk emphatically, indicating possessiveness. While in country, he would be watched, the dealer emphasized, tapping again. Should he decide to go against the request of the dealer, the dealer would know, the associates of the dealer would be told, he had said. Then, things would go sour.

Max and the dealer reached a gentleman's bargain that he would leave the country as soon as possible after purchase – even sooner than he had planned – despite his already possessing return tickets which were non-refundable. No matter. And with that out of the way, the dealer apparently satisfied with this agreement, Max brought out a large stack of bills from his bag, contained within a small white postal envelope, flap closed but unsealed and visibly bulging with its significant pecuniary burden. The dealer took the envelope, counting the currency for accuracy. wearing an absolutely blank expression. All of the bills were of the highest possible denomination.

Satisfied in full and finished counting after less than a minute had passed, the dealer smiled broadly, extending his hand which Max shook. We won't be seeing each other again, this lifetime, the dealer said with a glance, but thanked him for his commerce in the present.

Would Max like the crate? Max shook his head in the negative, opting instead for the small university-style shoulder bag that he had carried along to the meeting – wrapping the torment carefully inside of a spare shirt and secreting it in the bottom of his pack amidst assorted wet weather gear and travelling documents. Motioning that Max should show himself out, one last farewell was exchanged between the two men and then Max was out – out of the small sitting area, across the dark factory floor and back into the alley. Then, a motorized rickshaw hailed, back at a much quicker pace than he had arrived, out of the slum and into a more serviceable part of the city. Inside the bag, unbeknownst to him, the torment glowed with a sickening yellowish gleam.

PART 7

The outside of the hotel was in an uproar when Max returned, keeping one eye attentively on receiving back the proper change from the rickshaw driver whom he had just now renumerated and the other on the bustle of people on the sidewalk onto which he was about to expectorate himself. It appeared to be some sort of political protest, small in number, though the higher number of individuals who had appeared to counter the protestors had grown the overall size of persons crowding their way into the fracas considerably. Among these were the irate owners of the hotel themselves, claiming the protest area was under their jurisdiction by way of its location and that as such the location of the protest activity, hindering due commerce, constituted nothing less than a criminal offence. The protesters, proffering their own riposte in kind, argued that the walk constituted a public thoroughfare regardless to its proximity to any business, including that of the hotelier. The uniformed police that had appeared only a few minutes prior to Max's arrival had been sent to mediate however in the kingdom, as Max well knew, the favorable outcome would be ostensibly on the side of the businesspeople – unless the protest was somehow organized at the behest of the government itself, in one way or another.

As Max stepped off from the rickshaw and began to make his way through the crowd, which was directly blocking the front entrance, he saw out the corner of his eye a man who had without any doubt in his mind been in the back of the parade line earlier in the day at the intersection. Disconcerting coincidence at best Max thought to himself, though a definite indicator that professional force protection was indeed the man's particular line of work as per his previous suspicion. All the same, Max kept his head down, mouthing apologies soft-spokenly and to no one in particular as he made his way through the small crowd which, while inconvenient, seemed like an infinitesimal drop in the ocean compared to that which he had confronted during his morning journeys.

As he made his way through the crowd, through the double doors and then into the lobby the wife of one of the hoteliers stationed behind the counter barely noticed him, her gaze shifting nervously about at various goings-on in the scene taking place directly in front of the establishment, hoping that her husband had not bitten off more than he could chew. Max raised his hand in greeting in any case – force of habit – before turning down the corridor toward his room, the commotion outside all but forgotten as his mind turned monomaniacaly toward the immediate future and a chance alone with the torment.

Reaching his room he immediately noticed that the door was slightly ajar. His hackles raised, but not in overt alarm as of yet, given the precedence of generally poor state of upkeep he had witnessed during his brief but eventful stay thus far and the reputation of the area. Pushing the edge of the door slowly open with the tip of his shoe he was able to ascertain within several seconds that everything seemed to be as it should be – nothing apparently out of place, no signs of a partially hidden intruder within, no political protestor from outside taking sanctuary in the uninhabited space and utilizing his room

for whatever diverse purpose which would have without question caused him undue grief within the present schema. Content in the integrity of things Max closed the door behind him and sat down at last with the torment – drawing it carefully out of his satchel with shaking hands.

Now – finally – they two were alone. No nasty interfering dealer, no scenes, no protracted waiting periods in abject anxiety as he waited for his next contact, further instructions, in the pursuance of obtaining what was – he felt – by right – naturally his. Or rather, that he was its natural care-taker – for such items were not "owned" nor were they "purchased" – he had learned with some cynical amusement during those years which he had researched the item – and similar items – but no item was really similar to the torment, as his research had quickly shown him. Such items as these are, to paraphrase the natural terminology used by those several thousand miles farther east than he, only "borrowed." And as such, he had "borrowed" the item – but with a fee that would leave him on an entirely crippled income comparatively for the rest of the life. But then again, the torment itself might assist in rectifying that situation in the by and by, through hook or crook, for his pleasures were now her pleasures – his domiciles, her dwelling place.

The thought of his closeness to the torment brought him to a sudden state of sexual arousal, begging for release. He denied the instant urge, however, his need to cleanse himself from the acquired filth accumulated during the course of this day amongst days more pressing in his estimation, according to his sense of propriety. For he had all the time in the world ahead of him with the torment, an entire life to build with the demoness which lived within it, so he considered with no small degree of smugness. Those thoughts swirling pleasurably in his mind, he proceeded to stow the torment once again in the satchel – set right in the opening only, partially concealed, as his attentions would be upon it again very soon – then setting another set of clothing out upon the bed and proceeding to the shower.

As the veracity of the hot water capabilities of his lodgings had been previously established prior, Max commenced to set the water on full hot before stripping and placing his naked body under the faucet, though the pressure was, as before, not to his satisfaction. But no matter. The routine ritual did its trick well enough and, as ever, he had precedent for worse. The stream was able to wash off even the worse of the grime which had set upon him – the ever-present smog in the air, commingling with likewise ever-present sand from the surrounding deserts, impressed upon his flesh with the hot sweats of exertion and the cold sweats of dread which had assailed him physically at numerous points throughout his recent ordeal now drawing to a successful close.

The hot water sluiced down a body of a hardened nomad, thin but muscled and bearing the marks of one well-learned and even adept in the disciplines of privation both forced and brought down willingly. The musculature appeared for the most part to be that of someone somewhat naturally and genetically gifted, though seasoned with at least some regular acquaintance with manual labor and/or calisthenics of the more demanding military variety. Max had had his share of both, though the labor was of a sort done in the pursuit of his own peculiar and more than somewhat perverse private objectives and not for hire. He did avail himself of various schools of calisthenics and, as his physicality revealed, of the military sort – including forays into long-distance running – though his practices were without normative schedule and frequently interrupted by his travels abroad with brought with them their own sort of physical exertions, not easily dismissed.

As his cleansing winded down to a close he switched off the hot water and turned on to full cold for at least a minute, as was his usual routine in any part of the world regardless of the interior or exterior temperature of the landmass he happened to be inhabiting at the time, causing his muscles to draw taught and by effect accentuating the several small tattoos upon his flesh, coiling around an agitated tricep head – writing in a script not that of his birth nor parental heritage. These were his only markings, excepting a few small self-mulitatory wounds and the knicks and bangs of childhood – the latter, well faded and the former done in such a manner that they would not be readily identifiable as relating to their cause or intent should anyone have cause to examine.

Finished, Max towel-dried quickly but not thoroughly, trusting that the inherent dryness of the desert climate would do the trick quick enough even indoors. He walked naked back to the bedroom and once again removed the torment from its hiding place in the mouth of his satchel, slowly and somewhat sensuously unfurling the black shirt which had almost by accident seemed to wrap itself around its circumference during the course of his brief absence. The pewter casing around the glass shined hideously in the gleam of the overhead light, only matched by the hideous gleam of the sickening liquid within the torment which on cursory examination seemed to bear no discernible object within, in contrast to lesser amulets of somewhat similar make – the corpse oil in those cases usually having some setting – a figure usually, attached to the amulet base, given the appearance of an entity submerged at least partially within waters most foul.

He examined more closely, pulling the chair out from the battered wooden desk against the wall and sitting the torment upright in the fashion which he had been shown before by the dealer, the small prongs descending automatically to form a seating just as he had observed prior during the meeting in the warehouse. No, definitely not, Max thought to himself. There was no object within to be readily seen – though he could see some discolored specks here and there, blackish, floating within the liquid – miniscule enough to be indiscernible in the concourse of a cursory examination and more than like pieces of the pewter casing which had dislodged themselves into the liquid. But would that make any sense? For the roundish shape of the object, glass predominantly, seemed only to bear the pewter casing upon the outside, a partial exterior, he could see no points where the metal and liquid would intersect, insamuch as he could tell through staring through the exposed glass window, his face stationed only a few inches from its surface as he knelt down, still naked, peering into its shallow depths.

Staring at the torment his body suddenly become overcome with overtly sexual lust, waves of dark sensual energy suffusing him. His eyes still locked onto the torment he bent forward further on his knees, going in for an even closer look into the glass window of the amulet. His vision seemed to double and then triple and he began finding it it very hard to concentrate as the room around him became somewhat blurry – his exterior vision being replaced with hallucinations from within his mind, presenting themselves as bursts of color and image upon a backdrop of darkness. He saw the cult empress from the bloody procession in the slums, her eyes wide and watching him with naked threat – her skin taught and suffuse with black mania. Another vision, this time of the dealer after Max had left the warehouse, the small man sitting alone amidst the lone pool of light with the many thousands of dollars cash payment Max had supplied him with spread over the table – the dealer holding a closed fist over the currency and from tightly compressed fingers – the steady dripping of blood. And then a vision of the intelligence agents – the one likely Mossad, the other likely CIA or MI5 – converging on the hotel from different parts of the city. The man who had worked force protection for the procession and which he had also seen at the entrance to the hotel during the protest had been the one to bely his location. In fact, Max saw in his mind's eye, the man was sitting in a room in this very hotel – down the other corridor past the reception desk and lobby – his hand cradling a black landline telephone – passing information so that they could triangulate Max's position and coordinating the details of renditioning him when – later in the evening? In an hour's time?

Max began to sweat with horror as the sensual lust he had experienced turned to the ill and unmistakable effects of a flight-or-flight hormone dump. He knew in his guts that the visions he had seen were real – that they were coming for him, even now. Yet his body could not move though not for want of trying – he was paralyzed in a state beyond his own control, the contours of the torment in front of him visible for a few seconds then fading to black as his eyes involuntarily rolled back into their sockets as he entered back into the state of trance. At some point he realized that he was amidst all of this pleasuring himself, his sex having become erect to a severe degree brought on both by the initial lust and the horror that followed – one hand on his member and one hand wrapped around the edge of the seat of the chair upon which the torment sat, gripping the outrmost wooden spoke of the chair's back.

A piercing sensation overcame his mind, the feel of needles inserting themselves surgically into all sides of his skull and then at a moment when the pain became unbearable the feeling of his mind exploding into a million fragments – his consciousness soaring into pieces out into the horrid beyond of myriad star sytems while the blackness of the abyss entered within him. At that moment he regained his vision, the room once again becoming clear. He saw that his seed had spilled onto the dirty floor of the room but much more significantly that the torment seemed to be glowing – a disturbing, pulsating light coming from deep within it, the luminescence slowly becoming weaker. He grasped the torment and peered within the slowly fading light. Within, the light seeming to magnify the internal aspects of the mechanism within the corpse oil to some degree he saw with a sense of unparalleled revelation that there was a small entity visible inside of it. So miniscule that it would be barely discernible under normative circumstances but present all the same. It was a female figure – dressed from head to foot in a shining black alien fabric most resembling vinyl. Around that and partially concealing the stark curvatures of her body a cloak of a likewise unnatural manufacture, most similar to a thin black rubber but miraculously countouring to her brief movements with a pliancy which no mortal garment possessed.

His lips curled back in the manner of a fanatic's apprehension when he saw that her face was that of the girl he had seen in the procession earlier – though more mature – perhaps around twenty years of age in human years, though it was clear beyond a shadow of a doubt that the entity who was living within the torment was not human by any stretch of the imagination, though it may have been at some point, perhaps so far back that it was within a period of antiquity so obscure that it existed beyond any recorded history. The hair also was different – short, severe and combined with her attire indicating a profound will to dominate, a knowledge of the very heights of possible cruelty and the inborn devastating propensities of the most intense disciplinarian by nature.

She shifted ever so slightly – standing on nothing but suspended within the sickening viscosity of the corpse oil. Turning toward him, the entity stared – her eyes like two diamonds – emanating a radioactive light that threatened to burn like a nuclear Medusa the very retinas of those who stared into their unforgiving gaze too long. Her lips, reddish and thin, mouthed two words that sounded like klaxons within his mind.

"Go, now!"

HRAFNSSON

VII   SHAITAN

XIII   NYTHRA

XVII   NEMICU   ♀

For more of the artist's work, see his gallery:

HOF SÓLAR

serpentshrinesinistra.wordpress.com

THE END OF HATE IN THE LOVE OF THE KAINOS (ARCHAIOS) OPHIS

Matthew Wightman

The excitement of Violence—the thrill of exercising physical and mental dominance over a hated enemy; the delight of causing lasting and irreparable anguish to a trusted friend; the satisfaction of demonstrably wielding one's power over the inferior and superior alike; the willful violation of innocence; even the paradoxical potency to be found in the bittersweet pain of impotent rage; the transgression of all norms and values, including transgression itself; breaking the "Rule of Law;" living on the edge of extremes. Each of these experiences is essential to the life of the Sinister Satanist. Yet, to one unreflective, one for whom these can hardly be called genuine "experiences," one who cannot rightly be called sinister or satanic, they can also become a banal, obsessive and nihilistic prison, fitting of only the most pathetic of human dross.

The words that follow, like all words of *Ha-Satan*, are intended to disturb. Not to disturb the mundane, for whom the Spirit(s) of this article cares little, but to disturb those who claim allegiance to Disturbance—Evil, the Devil and the Sinister.

I strongly suspect that many who read the words that follow will Hate them. That's good. Hate is exactly what this article, and my Work in general, is about. I ask only that as you find yourself enraged by the words below that you reflect upon and confront the source of your indignation, that you ask yourself the difficult questions concerning the meaning and purpose of your Hate, even if it is a meaningless meaning and purposeless purpose that you find at the bottom of the bottomless abyss.

My hope is that the one who actively engages the words of this article will come to recognize the ultimate value in her otherwise empty contradictions—those actions and beliefs, those theses and antitheses, that cause her to circle perpetually around the hamster-wheel of meaning and meaninglessness from one poorly contrived synthesis to the next disappointing dissolution. My hope is that by actively confronting the dialectical nature of Nature, recognizing that all extremes, and thus all contradiction and opposition, merely turn back in upon themselves—toward submission and affirmation—the reader will be able to explore the borderless boundaries of her Hate sufficient to *fulfill* it, rather than remain perpetually trapped within the lifeless life of banal undeath.

Come then, on this journey through our Hate, the Source of our Greatest Power and, ultimately, our lowliest weakness.

How Do We Hate?

I preface the following words with the statement that, in general, I tend to favor those Satanists and occultists who emphasize action over reflection, as, for most of the 20th century, this emphasis was reversed, with a far greater focus being placed on a passive and academic approach to Ceremonial Magic, consisting largely of empty mental (and physical) masturbation.

Having said that, for some, the pendulum seems to have swung too far in the opposite direction so that what should be meaningful sinister action has become mindless banality and empty nihilism. What would once have been acts of genuine Sin, Evil or Transgression are now merely childish frat pranks, baseless elitism or petty acts of ego gratification given occult trappings after-the-fact so as to give some kind of social (Satanic) legitimacy to what is otherwise uninteresting sociopathic (mis)behavior.

As essential as radical *action* is to the life of the Satanist, it is *nothing* without meaningful *reflection* and sinister *intent*. To deny this is to be no better than the mindless dross despised by the Traditional Satanist, and, perhaps worse, is to make oneself lower than even the armchair occultists who feign serious commitment to the Sinister Dialectic through empty meandering. It is to dwell so thoroughly and thoughtlessly in the dirt that the blood becomes hardened by its clay, strangling the spirit (not an unattractive metaphor in a Qliphothic/Chthonic/Ahrimanic context, though I have yet to encounter even one capable of drawing sufficient meaning from this kind of meaninglessness, and, in the end, doing so only proves my point).

Without meaningful intent, there can be no *sinister* action, no antinomian transgression, no genuine opposition/rebellion or Radical Evil. Without thoughtful self-reflection, there can be only the banality of commonplace "evil"—actions found distasteful or unpleasant by the mundane masses without insight into the Darkness from which such actions originate (again, I am quite willing to explore the meaning even in this banality, and have done so in very practical ways on many occasions, but few are capable of such reflective unreflection, and, in the end, it leads to the same place). Such thoughtless actions are those of a simpleminded and sub-conscious animal, unworthy of the Sinister Nature of the Dark Gods who will not even deign to look upon the one who enacts them with contempt or amused pity, let alone favor.

The Sinister Philosophies of Traditional Satanism have always emphasized personal evolution, growth and the pedagogical benefits of dangerous and painful transgressive action. Even if this evolution ultimately yields something bestial and alien whose thought and logic are inimical to human consciousness, such a state is necessarily achieved through conscious acts, sinister intellect and deep empathy. That is to say that the actions of the Sinister Satanist are always intended to be *meaningful* and *intentional*—before, during and after the act; as if an act otherwise considered "evil" or "transgressive" means nothing to the one who acts—as a wolf eating a lamb or an obese mundane gulping down a double-cheese burger—it lacks all *sinister* character. Such acts are neither human nor inhuman, neither moral nor immoral, but only non-human (or too human) and non-moral. Such acts are without Evil and are in no respect Transgressive. Neither can such acts truly be called dangerous or painful in any but the most mundane of ways. Actions of this kind are surd, given meaning only by those who have judged them externally without the understanding and empathy that the True Satanist is called to cultivate. One who acts without such understanding is a mere human-animal slave to her obsessive-compulsive impulses, the very definition of the societal dross despised by the Traditional Satanist. Indeed, to engage in such unthinking violence is to put oneself beneath even the mental masturbation of the armchair Satanist, and is thus of utter disinterest to the Dark Gods.

The emphasis on thoughtless action through blind authoritarian submission and emotional dissociation of many of today's "satanic elite" represents a fundamental break with the Sinister Tradition, with those espousing it sharing little in common with the Sinister Antiheroes of History and far more in common with the spoiled emo-rich-kid enslaved to his stunted maturity because mommy and daddy didn't pay enough attention to him, driving him to prey on those more vulnerable than himself in hopes that someone will turn even a revolted eye in his direction, or the petty drug dealer enslaved to the poverty of his birth and the blow up his nose, the priestly pedophile enslaved to the urges of his theologically repressed ego, or the average-Joe racist enslaved to the ignorance of his heritage and circumstances of his society. There is nothing "elite" or "sinister" about these individuals or their actions, evidenced by their mindless repetition of violence without growth or personal evolution, with any Satanic trappings added merely as a vain attempt to give profundity to otherwise banal cruelty.

Having the deepest respect for the work of David Myatt, for whom there seems sufficient evidence to identify as the original "Anton Long," recognizing that his "call to action" was genuine, well timed, and, for those who took his words seriously, clearly every bit as fulfilling and deeply meaningful as he promised, it must be acknowledged that this is only true because he has had thoughtful reflection and meaningful intention covered. In addition to a willingness to act in the presence of the dangers of this world and that which lies beyond and beneath, Myatt possesses a sharp intellect, an empathic heart and the ability for thoughtful reflection and eloquent articulation. He has not acted purely on base instinct (though this too has been immanently present and finely honed) or unreflective Hatred (despite it being essential to his vision up to and through its fulfillment) but has been able to conjoin meaningful action with equally meaningful intention, reflection and articulate communication. To divorce these is not to find freedom or power but only further slavery and impotence, regardless of whatever satanic "street-cred" or "edginess" one feels doing so offers.

Why Do We Hate?

Among those lessons learned during my years of pursing the Nietzschean Will to Power through meaningful action is *that there is no more Power to be found within the "Will to Power" than there is to be found in the relationship between the Master and her Slave, the Sadist and a Masochist or the Priest and his Sacrifice.* The Power to be found in the Will to Power can be likened to the emptiness of the narcissist's egotistical self-love, which is, in reality, the self-loathing of a shattered and helpless ego, one powerless to overcome itself because, despite outward appearances of arrogant confidence, it is overcome by fear.

So long as you pursue the "Will to Power" you will always be a Slave to that Will—the Will of The Magian All-Power. That is to say, as long as you pursue the Will to Power as the End of All means, exactly as Nietzsche (and the Hebrews) insisted that All must, you will fail to achieve Power, and will lose your will, just as Nietzsche and many before and after him ultimately have. The same is true of Sadism and the Hatred that fuels it, which ultimately find their source and are grounded in the Narcissistic Fear of the Absolute Other—the indifferent Creator after whose passion (Love or Hate) is desperately, though often unconsciously or secretly, sought, with the hope of escaping, through violence and/or submission, the turmoil of simultaneous revulsion and obsession with the Magian All-Power. It is only by acknowledging our slavery, by accepting our bondage and relinquishing the Will to Power that we can hope to reclaim our power from the Will and our will from Power.

There will never be enough corpses to pile, enough skulls to stack, enough blood in which to drench the fields or enough tears to fill the dried-up oceans of the scorched Earth to satisfy the bottomless depths of your Hate or fulfill your unquenchable desire for Power (and acceptance by Power)—for Sadistic Domination over All. The reader, if she has truly committed sinister acts, knows this to be true in the depths of her Black Heart. She experiences it each time the thrill of the last act of torture or sacrifice has ended, when the screams of terror have gone silent and the blood has dried, in the emptiness of solitude and longing to return to the "Temple" or "Altar" again, just as the drug or sex addict craves the next high or dissolution of orgasm.

Just as Sade continued to pull back the masks of Power through his ever escalating and inventive sadism—each time expecting to find himself free of, by and in it (fully possessing and possessed by it)—only to discover yet another expression of that indifferent and unaccountable Power always beyond his cum and blood-drenched grasp, and thus always further enslaved to Its terrible and indifferent Will, there will *always* be One more Powerful, more indifferently hateful, before whom you are *nothing*, unworthy of even a momentary thought amidst Eternity...and yet you are *everything* that the One has always-already decided that you will be, despite of yourself.

You will never cause that One enough pain—indeed, you will never cause It *any* pain at all—to satisfy your Black Heart, you will never shed enough blood of Its Chosen meek—about which It ultimately does not care either, despite their desperate protestations otherwise—never achieve enough Power to satisfy your will against Its (nor turns Its Will toward yours), and so long as you refuse to accept this, so long as you continue to strive and oppose yourself—the only real obstacle to yourself—you will forever be the slave of your Self—the Master that does not even notice your labor let alone your struggle to resist It. You will perpetually fail to achieve the sinister end that you seek and earn only the indifference of the Dark Gods whom you so desperately desire to impress.

In your rebellion, in your defiance, in your sin and the depths of your Cold Hate—beyond the Fires of your tumultuous Rage—of all that stands in your way, in your Desire for Unlimited and Unaccountable Power, in the fantasy of seeing that Power unleashed upon your Enemy—to turn the Attention of Its Cold and Indifferent Rejection of you to *you*—and ultimately in the Freedom that you expect to find in so doing, you will discover yourself more unwittingly obedient, more fearful, more rejected, more unnoticed, more unsatisfied and more enslaved at each and every turn. And when you have been used up, when the emptiness of the perpetual dialectic finally ceases to sustain you—and make absolutely no mistake, it *will* cease to sustain you, as the potency of its power is finite—you will be discarded by the Dark Gods—for They care not for empty failures. There will be no appreciation for your past sacrifices, no awards given for your exhaustive effort—the Dark Gods do not bestow "participation trophies;" They care only for those capable of fulfilling Their Will, for

what you do for Them NOW and can do for Them in the future in bringing about that fulfillment. One so trapped by the fear of death, dissolution and of being forgotten that she refuses to fulfill the End of Hate by taking sinister action to its own dissolution is of no use to Them and will only ensure that she meets her fated fear as They turn Their attention to those younger, stronger and potentially more likely to fulfill Their purposes than she, in her pathetic "undeath," can offer.

Though the perpetual denial of your *jouissance*, the permanently elusive fulfillment of your desire, might sustain you—in your emptiness—for a time (just as Lacan observed that it does for the vast majority of mundanes), and while it may temporarily hold the attention of the Dark Gods, hopeful that you might finally muster the strength and courage to do what is necessary while it lasts, should you ultimately fail to do so, your life will be one of meaningless suffering and hollow, unfulfilling accomplishment; more hollow than the lowest and pathetic failure, ending only in the shallowness of the pit and leaving behind nothing but nameless ashes, bitter memories for those few foolish enough to care about you and the utterly indifferent laughter of your Enemy—Eternally, yet completely unknowingly, dancing upon your unmarked and forgotten grave to the satisfaction of Its always-already fulfilled—with or without you, who are nothing to It—Glory.

It is to this bleak vision that you have to look forward should you refuse to accept that the turmoil of your heart, the sinister acts of violence and sadistic Hate, are a means to and not the End (a tragically (un)necessary means, each paradoxically moving you further and further from that End) and that to truly win the favor of the Dark Gods, you must do what they are only able to do through you—fulfill Their End.

You may believe that by creating Hell on Earth, both for yourself and others, that you have done more than accept the turmoil, having embraced it fully, and will, therefore, be fittingly blessed by the Gods for all Eternity (with further welcomed pain). However, if you have not yet taken it a step further, if you have not seen Hell through to its Endless End, if you have found yourself stymied by repetitive acts of violence and the perpetual desire to repeat the same sacrifices of escalating sadism over and over again like an obsessive compulsive—just as the minds and actions of the Marquis de Sade and Nietzsche vainly struggled against at the end of their lives—you will always have failed to Overcome, failed to truly Hate enough, failed to be Radically Evil, Sadistic or Transgressive, and you will thus always and forever be without power or significance. The Dark Gods have no use for such failures and will turn their visages from your empty husk when they have finished with you, denying you even the attention of their ire; they will provide you with none of the welcomed pain that reminds you of your continued existence in hollow unlife, for They care and are concerned only about those with purpose, with value, capable of Fulfilling Their Sinister Agenda against the Magian All-Power.

The Philosophies of Sade and Nietzsche (as well as Foucault and Derrida) are NOT, despite popular (and ignorant) opinion, in any way nihilistic, *unless* they are denied their fulfillment. By living in the struggle of perpetual contradiction—defined by the violent pursuit of Power over that which is Hated—without accepting the fullest consequences of the contradiction's resolution—when one must turn that Hatred in upon Itself—one will only serve the Will of the Hated—the Magian All-Power—serving to achieve less and less power until she is reduced to a recyclable impotence to be consumed and churned back into the Magian Matrix—for the Dark Gods to whom you no longer hold interest will abandon you to the Magian Creator who has even less interest in (or care for) you.

When/Where Do We Hate?

The reflections of this section will be the shortest and most mysterious in that the answer to when and where we Hate will likely only be discovered by the reader in hindsight, as she comes to see that there truly is a fulfillment—a Telos—of Hate, pointing back to its acausal Beginnings.

If we allow ourselves to take our Hate to its Ultimate End in the bittersweetness of meaningful action, as we are called to do by both Sinister Satanism and the Dark Gods, we will finally achieve that for which Hate was ultimately intended. The failure to do so is to falter in sinister action and remain forever a slave to the Magian All-Power.

I strongly suspect that if you engage the truth of these words through whatever means you are called to do so—a single, though prolonged, multifaceted and complex act of Empathic Sadism, Self/Other-Sacrifice and profound Intimate Betrayal was my own Path to Perdition/Salvation (which was, of course, preceded by years of active preparation, study and reflection)—you will find that the End of Hate is a definitive moment that has always been present; that, in fact, all of those Hateful and/or Transgressive acts of Sacrifice and Sadism were both a shamefully unnecessary hindrance to your growth and Self-Overcoming *and* the only means by which *you*, in your shame—in your helpless prison within the dialectic—*could* grow; each calling you to acknowledge and accept the Nightmare of Abraham *and* the Nations, the Reconciliation of Hate with Love in the Endless Freedom of the Life of Deathless Death in Omn/I(m)potent Peace.

Who/What Do We Hate?

The deep-seated desire, the obsessive need among Sinister Satanists—and those occultists otherwise influenced by Sinister Thought—to escape the Magian / Demiurgic/ Semitic / Abrahmaic/ Hebraic / Kabbalistic / Judeo-Christian Mythos, Logos, Law and Logic is a laudable goal to which I have thus far dedicated my entire life.

It is also an *Impossible* goal to achieve.

I do not use the term "impossible" lightly or as hyperbole. I mean, quite literally, that there is absolutely no means at our, or Their, disposal, no region of existence (or non-existence), no dark corner of consciousness, sub-consciousness or unconsciousness, no language (or silence), no mythology, no law or logic that is not always-already possessed (in)completely by the Magian All-Power. After all, all power (including the absence of power) is not only derived from the Magian Creator, it *is* the Magian Creator.

The sooner that those reading these words come to accept this truth, the sooner they will find themselves free to pursue Their Ends.

I will not spend the remainder of this article seeking to convince you of this simple fact as it would take only a cursory investigation into the origins of the human species and our behavioral modernity, the ancient tribes and the earliest civilizations and religions of Earth, the development of human language and written alphabets, the migration patterns of both DNA and language, to reveal how utterly interdependent the human species (and even those other hominid species long since absorbed into our own) is.

As a minor example, I adjure any interested reader to take a closer look at the origin and migration patterns of the Northern Europeans—whose mythology has long been an illusory source of hope for many Sinister Satanists—or the influence of the Semitic Phoenicians on the Hellenistic Greeks and Egyptians—two other favored cultures.

Never mind the fact that returning to some pure form of a "philosophy of the ancients" has been made impossible by later intermingling of the sociolinguistic associations that we have come to inherit as the building blocks of our modern consciousnesses, careful study will reveal that this intermingling had always-already happened—a study of Northern Africa, pre-historic Israel, Jordan and Turkey (and, from there, Russia, Scandinavia, India, Eastern Asia and the Americas) would likely prove quite illuminating in this regard.

True, there are languages and systems other than those explicitly grounded in Jewish Kabbalah to which the Sinister Satanist can appeal, but these systems are also less able to deal directly with the Magian contamination present within them, having obfuscated the problem with less overt language and having renamed the Essence of the Creator, the Magian All-Power, with more subtle and innocuous terms (e.g. "The Will to Power"). In this respect, these "pure" systems have only hidden the depths of their impurity, thereby making them far more dangerous to those who seek liberation from the Magian Essence.

Perhaps that has been the "sinister" goal all along, to penetrate the hearts and minds of the enemies of the Semitic Demiurge, ensuring their unending slavery and unwitting (yet willing) submission—for, after all, who is ultimately more sinister than Yahweh? By giving the Magian All-Power more palatable Names and Associations (far fewer Satanists fear and despise Týr or Kronos as they do Yahweh), the Sinister Satanist only sustains the Magian reach. Neither Pseudoscience nor Pseudohistory (including personal pseudohistories) will save us from this reality; they will only deepen our unwitting dependence upon it.

It is for this reason that I have engaged in several Insight Roles, each spanning years, coming to live and think as those I Hated, for only by understanding them, by speaking and imagining the world like them, by coming to Love them, and, indeed, by *becoming* them, could I truly fulfill my Hatred against them.

The bitter irony is that most of what is labeled as "Hardcore" or "Extreme" Satanism, especially of today's "Wamphyric" kind, is, more often than not, simply repackaged Jewish Yahwehism, down to its characteristic obsessive sadomasochism and elitist separatism, making the new "sinister elite" the very epitome of everything that these individuals claim to Hate. And while doing so is indeed the final stage to True Overcoming, these "Satanists" seem to have yielded to their fear, just as their Jewish counterparts have for millennia (giving credence to the old refrain that the world is made of only two groups: "Jews" and "Heretical Jews"). They have chosen to remain inert in the repetitive banality of their own hell, learning nothing transgressive from the experience of Self-Othering and satisfying themselves only temporarily by "shocking" the easily disturbed mundane world around them.

The words of these supposed "extremists" and "dissidents" (who are only recapitulating the same boring conformity and order) are just as easy to deconstruct in their inner contradiction as those of the despised Hebrews and every bit as dependant upon empty metaphysical claims that are ultimately rather poor attempts to obfuscate fear, and control those of weak will. Such individuals exhort their members to "overcome" and "conquer" while demanding blind, unthinking obedience and a hardened heart (and mind) that make true sinister action impossible; they laud the "Will to Power," yet simultaneously demand the attitude of an obsequious slave to a Power that is even *more* enslaved to Itself. And, worst of all, they never move beyond this place of utter vanity. They never gain any *insight* from the role. A tragic shame, as they are so close (yet so far away), from the very edge of taking sinister action to its conclusion through the Fullest Embrace of Hate, yet always denying themselves the final act of fulfillment out of fear.

This is, of course, the Orwellian dilemma created by an active embrace of "doublethink," the state of unyielding resistance to the inevitable and unavoidable deconstruction of inner contradiction made known to the one who practices it by intense cognitive dissonance (though it is designed to ease this dissonance, it

will *always* fail to do so) and (often unconscious) emotional turmoil of the perpetually dying mind. It is to exist in a state of endless failure and frustration (Hell) yet always obsessively driven by a (false and feared) hope of fulfillment.

Such an "undead" state would *almost* be admirable if it were actually capable of serving any meaningful purpose beyond banal self-effacement, or if it were truly any different from those mundane theologies and philosophies that have vainly sought to stave off the End of Life in Death through childish metaphysics promising perpetual existence—the great irony of which is that had any of these frightened children actually accepted and embraced the End, had they *fulfilled* their lives rather than fearfully attempting to hoard them away from death, they, and we, might not now be on the precipice of all life's end and the realization of their very fear.

True, such perpetual self-denial can sustain the life of a community (and, to a lesser extent, an individual) *almost* indefinitely, as it has for Jews and those who emulate them (Christians, Muslims, most everyone else, etc.), but it is an empty life of meaningless undeath, of slavery and failure that will not only fail to turn the attention of the Gods for all but a moment, but will, ultimately, come to the very conclusion it fears. Such individuals seek to string along the interest of the Dark Gods with the perpetual hope that they might finally have the insight and courage to fulfill Their End, but inherent to this philosophy is a perpetual failure to do so (a *seemingly* endless end characterized by an empty sadomasochism that is ultimately of no interest to the Dark Gods in its banality). This is made even more pitiable by the fact that not only are these "Satanists" incapable of fulfilling their own aims, but that such failure is knowingly (yet willfully forgotten) essential to their pathetic existence: they depend upon remaining trapped within the commonplace, unwilling and unable to fulfill their Sinister Hatred (yet insisting upon pursuing it) as well as incapable of achieving the power after which they lust yet perpetually deny themselves out of fear. They exhort members to action with the threat of the Undead Gods' ire, or, worse, indifference, at failure; yet, failure is the *only* promise that can be made—as it is essential to the philosophy—as is the Undead Gods' ultimate disinterest in them.

Yes, a great deal can be learned from acts of sadomasochism, both from the perspective of the Sadist and the Masochist, and yes, there is even more to be learned by becoming One with Hate—by becoming One with the Hated—but if anything is to be *learned* from this dialectic, if there is to be anything other than the perpetual undeath of remaining trapped within the dialectic (by futilely hoping to trap the dialectic within) until one's *inevitable* dissolution—which is nothing more than an obsessive (and mundane) fear of death—it is that the dialectic is a *means*—a profoundly *unnecessary* means, only *made* necessary by Magian Society's acausal inscription of our consciousness into its metaphysics at the moment of our conscious emergence into the world, which constantly seeks to reassert itself upon any with the insight to bypass its stranglehold—not the *End* to personal transformation, to truly achieving that which claims to be sought after, and thus to remain trapped within the spirals of the dialectic serves no meaningful purpose and is utterly unworthy of the Dark Gods' (or True Satanist's) attention.

Equally true is that although the uneasy doublethink described above can be an effective tool to control the unthinking masses toward sinister ends, for a time, and, I suppose, one might find a certain romantic nobility in the brilliant mind and iron will willingly and knowingly submitting itself to the endless torment of perpetually unfulfilled desire of the cognitive and emotional dissonance of Self-Contradiction (Vindex)—a philosophy made popular by 90s Vampire Novellas and George Lucas' portrayal of the Sith—when one acknowledges that this is also to perpetually and

meaninglessly fail to achieve one's Ends because she has become so fearfully obsessed with what are ultimately unnecessary *means*, the Satanist stands at the Crossroads of further fear and failure (ultimately leading to her demise at the hands of her "friends" and indifferent Enemy) and True Overcoming.

At this point the Satanist has the choice between persisting in repetitive nihilistic action that is forever denied its fulfillment because she fears its End, leading her to perpetual, slothful inertia of empty and meaningless self-conflict and ultimately unremarkable dissolution—a banal and uninteresting fate deserved only by the lowliest dross and armchair occultists, and of absolutely no interest to the Dark Gods—or she can actually *learn* something from her actions that will lead her to the very state of consciousness that she desires, the ultimate stateless state that the Dark Gods themselves represent and revere, where one's actions have become truly Other.

The former will be the fate of the modern "undead elite" unless it learns to accept the *meaning* of the cognitive dissonance that it has rightly cultivated—that the overcoming motivated by the 'Martinet' and 'Discipline' of sinister action must itself be Overcome through deep and meaningful reflection—ultimately yielding peace, freedom, love, joy and strength in the deathless death of power-lessness (a lesson that Myatt seems to have learned and articulated well in recent years).

How Do We Love?

Having said all of this, having stirred the pot as it were, having forced uncomfortable reflection and hopefully equally uncomfortable action, it seems to me that there *is* something to developing a Satanic system without overt Semitic underpinnings that both recognizes the fundamental reality of all that has been said above, but which, with open eyes, seeks to undercut it, nevertheless knowing the inescapability of Demiurgic Reality (I tend to read the MSS of the ONA in this way, but it is somewhat doubtful that this was the initial intent and, even if it were, it has obviously been difficult for most to maintain consistently).

To this end, the end of this article serves as an introduction to the beginning of just such a project; one that benefits from the overt tools and insights learned from Christian and Jewish practice and theology, and its derived antithesis, Qliphothic Kabbalah, but which translates those tools and insights into a system of constantly shifting symbolism, one founded upon elusive and perpetually deconstructing language that seeks to evade all obstructions leading to its End(s).

Beyond my ongoing work on the *Kitvei Kodesh HaChol*, grounded in the Hebraic (Klifotic) Mythos, and the Monographic Grimoire series of the recently established *Empty Temple, Tomb and Throne* (the ET3), I intend to develop a series of works grounded in the mythos of the Kainos (Archaios) Ophis (the New (Old) Serpent) that will draw from other mythologies, especially those of post-modern horror, atheistic/materialistic scientism, Hellenistic, Scandinavian/Celtic/Norse traditions (my own heritage) and those of Native American and Pre-Columbian civilizations. It is my hope that those who find any system openly influenced by Semitic language and Hebraically derived symbolism a stumbling-block will find this work more accessible and palatable to their sensibilities. What will follow, however, is only the practical unfolding of all that has already been said, in brief, above.

Kainos (Archaios) Ophis

Contrary to the mythology of our ancestors, the Beginning was not characterized by Chaos. In fact, the Beginning was Perfect Order—Even, Uniform, Unified, Potent and Passionate—begging for the excitement of Imbalance, Separation, Lusting for Hate, the thrill of Violence, and ultimately exploding in the "Big Bang"—the ferocious explosion of energy that initiated the Creation of Time and Space, as well as the moment at which Chaos, characterized by unevenness, imbalance and inequality was born.

Power (and Order) was concentrated in some places and void in others; hot and cold, fast and slow, light and darkness became meaningful categories as distinction became the essential reality. Power became the fundamental currency of the Universe, moving from greater concentrations to lesser in an unthinking redistribution of power downward.

Life, though depending upon and obeying the very same laws of power's downward redistribution, reversed the prior (dis)order by vampirically drawing energy from its environment—living and non-living—to create an imbalance capable of temporarily hoarding power within an individual.

The result has been both wonderful and horrific, as life has manifested creatures capable of not only sentient (acausal) self-awareness of the Universe's downward redistribution of power and life's inherent vampirism that seeks to trap power within the individual, but also a system of symbolic language and values that both depend upon *and* fundamentally contradict these foundational realities of its existence.

Human awareness comes to find deeper and often more ethereal distinctions within existence, such that life and death, pleasure and pain, love and hate, good and evil become equally meaningful to light and darkness or power and impotence. This leads our ancestors to find value in individual life, first, at a family and then tribal level, but eventually spanning out into the infinite (and non-living), from the single-celled organism (or smallest molecule), to the whole of existence and every individual and collective in between; while at the same time, the truth that in order for one to survive and thrive another must necessarily perish at the hands of the survivor is inescapable.

This contradiction and the cognitive dissonance that it creates has led to all manner of resentment and self-delusions aimed at easing or embracing said resentment—whether they be of the "Sky Daddy" or "Undead God" variety—grounded in metaphysical masturbation and eschatological escapism that promises to make everything "alright." Time and again these delusions are revealed for what they are; not by some external force, not by a prophet of the True God, but by the very inherent instability of the symbolism that grounds and sustains them. Their demise comes from within. In a word, they are torn apart by the inherent (anti)force of *deconstruction*.

Yet, the violent Chaos of our existence has a Telos, driven by the Arrow of Time, which leads ultimately to the Eternally (un)Fulfilled Entropic Equilibrium that will be the End of Time and Space. Like the Beginning, the End will be Even, Uniform, Balanced and Equal. Yet, unlike at the Beginning, in the End, All Power will be impotent, cold, dull and unusable. The finite usable power of Infinite Power will have reached its end in the limitless unusable power of cold heat at Heat Death.

As there was in the Beginning, in the End there will be peace, but unlike the hot, uncomfortable peace of the Beginning, that which Lusted in anticipation of War and the Conflict of Imbalance, the End will be without hope of Violence or Aggression as all lust and hate cool into inert and impotent *somethingness*—somethingness that will look identical to *nothingness* in the inability of any to distinguish or differentiate between All and None—Eternal and Unknowable Equality will have been achieved.

That which was impossible at the moment of Creation's emergence and made even more so as Life became fully conscious—thereby deepening the symbolic distinction between the powerful and powerless—the True Reconciliation of Opposites, the Fulfillment of Separation and Unity, Transcendence and Immanence, Hate and Love, Good and Evil, Power and Impotence, Light and Darkness will have become the Inevitable and Eternal End. The Hell (and Heaven) of Yahweh and Satan will be at Hand. The All-Power will have been fully diminished, utterly defaced; yet it will be made even more all-embracing. For the first time, genuine freedom from and within Power will be not only possible, but also actual and universal.

Do not think this End in "death" deprives our present, past or future of its meaning, for if one follows the admonishments of this essay to Their End, she will find that the opposite is true.

The mystery that I share with you today is that we do not have to wait until the banal "heat death" of our universe to experience genuine freedom (a good thing, considering that neither we nor any other form of life will be around to experience that physical end) and that, indeed, it has always-already been achieved by the One alone able to achieve it, ensuring that, in fact, we *will* be (are, and always have been) present to experience it.

Hidden in the human experience, in our symbolic language, our alphabets, the myths, metaphors and even metaphysics of our conscious lives, is the cipher for understanding, accepting, reconciling, overcoming and, if one has the courage, fulfilling not only all oppositional distinctions—all theses and antitheses—but all syntheses as well. It is the One (that is also All, Many/Some and None) (un)deconstructable symbol that, in its very Essenceless Essence, *is* deconstruction, *is* the (un)fulfillment of Entropy, is the true achievement of "post-structuralism" as the One Structureless Structure, Foundationless Foundation—the Fullness of Emptiness and the Fulfillment of the Deferral of Différance—that not only frees the (All)-Power trapped within the stilted dialectic of the perpetual life of death and (un)death of life, but which allows All to live a life of (im)perfect love by the (in)complete power of the Spirt(s) of some-power (a true pagan revival), genuinely accountable to No-Power and ultimately promising true and eternal deathless life (an impossible possibility).

It is an open secret, hiding everywhere, in plain sight, though (un)intentionally obscured by the metaphysics of the Magian/Sinister Dialectic, from the moment of our first breath to our last.

I leave it to each reader to uncover this Truth on her own, through meaningful action, as my stating it outright in words any further is likely only to darken her vision before she has achieved True Understanding. Nevertheless, given honest and active commitment, the kind of commitment demanded by Traditional Satanism and the Dark Gods, this Understanding will be achieved, leading one to recognize the manner in which the Dialectic finds its conclusion—the fulfillment of Sadism, Hatred, Satanic Rebellion *and* the Magian All-Power, along with Empathy, Love, Faithful Obedience and the Numinous.

At the moment of Revelation, one will bear witness to a New "Big-Bang" created by the Synthesisless Synthesis of All and None, resigning all of her hate, evil, sadism and sinful transgression to a grateful, penitent, sorrowful, joyful and wonderful mourning of the profane past—the death of the Magian All-Power and the cessation of the unlife of Its (un)Holy Dialectic—as she moves forward in love, peace, joy and freedom into a New and Eternally Fulfilled Future.

The only question is, do *you* have the courage to face what even the Devil and the Creator cannot? To go where Angels and Demons refuse to tread because doing so would mean no longer being, and yet being for the very first time, Other than the Hate that they have always *been* and fear to *be* without? Do you Hate enough? Can you take your Hate "all the way" such that it also becomes your Love—and your Love your Hate—and, if so, can you dwell so totally in the moment of contradiction and doublethink, without retreat, without drawing oneself back up into the dialectic or the dialectic back up into oneself, that the fear and logical error dissolve, deconstructing themselves in the ultimate act of (Self)-Sacrifice, leaving behind not the dreadfully expected barren nihilism, not the emptiness of the last unfulfilling orgasm or high, but a deeper and richer meaning and freedom capable of sustaining Itself through both the Horror and Wonder of the Sinister and Numinous, and well Into and Beyond the Synthesisless Synthesis of them Both?

This is what the Kainos (Archaios) Ophis represents. A New Old Testament of Creation that fulfills the Old *and* the New to yield something that is both familiar and yet never before possible: True Love, Peace, Strength, Joy and Freedom in the Eternal Life of Deathless Death.

ABERRATIONS OF A DRAGON
Raze Books

I

They who walked these shores
As shadows in our past
Met a foreign man
Cloaked in robes of blood
Who spoke in a tongue
Too close to their own.
"As sure as candles drip wax
When burning through the night
Staining the wood upon which it cools,
So too must you pay
A due for the refuse of your existence."
The Man in Red whispered strong
While dropping globes of waning power
Into the churning waters
Of the river that fed children
And women alike.
"So I have called you to this land,
To begin this payment."
Cowering in fear of their god paying witness
They step forward, arms extended.
Gripped by a pristine hand from the cloak of red
Water drips onto their palm.
"So now in your town upon the water
You will know where your wax falls,
For you have sold your soul
For drops of water."
The Man Cloaked in Red gripped a sphere
Within which swirled hues
Of both red and purple
That betrayed a world
Of treason and sin.
Only to be released
Like the goat of Azazel
Into the churning waters unknown
Never to be seen again.

II

Tributaries, calloused and torn
Wretched fingers that reached
Into the innards
Of people unsuspecting
So that they too
Confronted in strides
Could let loose a slew
Of regret and retribution
To feed the god of this land
Spreading grass
In directions entire
That once fed meat
And bone
Now has dried
To a crisp point
So that the horizon
Brightening
Could be seen as a wave
Of dead and dying things
Never again did they return to this land.

III

I have travelled lands wet and dry
Listened upon the boughs only to witness genocide
Waves have felt my hull in jarring strokes
And I've seen lands of sand and salt
Lands where people are called blokes
and where names remain ever yet unheard
But even yet, this hollow song plays,
whistling around the frame of my body
Driving me up walls and to rake my claws
And no matter how often I look up, it's still cloudy
To find solace in my mind yet again
I retreat to the halls of a faith
That I left at home when I boarded that train
Aged wood supports me after these years of searching
Simple words litter my thoughts before merging
Into these few lines:
"Fresh spots of rain
litter the stained glass
as the resolve of a man,

lost adrift in the sea,
breaks itself down
in this hollow place"

IV

Slip ups as I fall down slopes
That I thought I knew
So I stumble up this height
To find my goal to have dried up
No flags or trees mark the spot
Only dried
Cracked
Ground infested with weeds
Of opium and lily
Scattered sunlight through thin clouds,
Built by an artifice of power,
And metal,
Casting deep shadows on all that surround
But upon my shoulders
No shadow touches the ground
I awake to find
I still sleep alone

V

I look at these hands
Cracked and creviced
Tattooed with scars deeper than skin
I slip my fingers between yours
So we can walk together
Off this beaten path
Words hang between us unseen
In quiet strides
Making our way through sentinels of trees
A wind in the firmament
Singing tree songs obscuring our listless walk
On this cloud stricken day
Moss populated log in dry leaved hedge
To support the weight
Of our acts in our nightly forgotten endeavors
A soft hum
Running water distance
A lie to ensorcell our interest

In a long dried river
When the long lost ones
Spoke with He Cloaked in Red Robes

VI

Afternoons slipping into tomorrows
Sky high blues flecked with reds
As our day ends
I sit and wait
At nights, alone
For you
As an apparition
To haunt my dreams
Tremors in the night
As I stutter into
Open eyes
To find:
You were never here
Broken hearted
Scatter
As I meander into your arms
A pilgrim
To the Mecca of your heart
Lighted lips have painted me a Fool
To be Hung at the mount of your helm
Wolves held at bay
As I hear what you say
Wilted sunflowers
Litter our panes of glass
As drops of rain
Pelt the packed snow
In our abode
That hugs a long dried river

VII

Reactionaries visible
As artifices of terror
Become erect against
A slowly darkening horizon
Rants and spittle
To sway those affected
From the swoon of this god

Whom was too close
Too Imminent
A god they once feared
Forsaken
For a power they can see
And feel
As their lands run dry
And shapes gather
At the edge of the forest
There
The Man Cloaked in Red waits

THE LICH: UNDEATH & THE NATURE OF TRANSFIGURATION

Somnus Dreadwood

LICH. The very word is shrouded in lore and misinformation, though is in fact a state of being that every disciple of the black path should aspire to attain in one form or another. Consider for a moment what you know about this term. Most individuals upon reading that singular word think of adolescent fantasy stories and games. Their minds gravitate to the realm of fiction rather than the reality of one of the most terrifying beings to ever have left its dark mark upon this earthly plane called Etheris. What few realize is that the Lich is very real and very much an absolute defiant terror that spits in the face of nature, divinity and the filth of the Judeo-Christian-Islamic theological stranglehold. The Lich is a horror from the Eternal Grave; an abomination that is cold, calculated, powerful, patient and absolutely immortal. The Lich is not only a being of undeath in the truest definition, but an animated, intelligent and malevolent promise of a future everlasting in a state of perpetual biological and metaphysical stasis augmented and bolstered by the unforgiving current of death.

To understand this concept of an unliving monster that once identified itself as a mortal being, you first have to understand how this whole aspect of being first came to exist. The origins of the word can be traced to various European languages where their linguistic term simply translated to "corpse". In the Maergzjiran Cabal, it was initially the German "Leiche" due to the Grandmistress of the era being of German descent and simply utilizing that term to mask the truly wicked creature that dared to overcome mortal boundaries.

By virtue of the name itself, "corpse", and owing to the nature of it returning, we immediately turn our attention toward the necromantic arts.

However, while necromancy will offer you the opportunity to speak with the dead, throw death curses and grant you some of the natural aspects of death while being fully alive, necromancy was devoid of any reference to becoming a Lich through the rites of Lichdom. Certainly, many necromancers sought immortality and few achieved it through pacts, siphoning the spirit of others, or through vampirism, what fundamentally changes the nature of this type of immortality was the use of the phylactery. This was and still remains the absolute trigger object and infallible key to necromantic transfiguration; that is, undeath apotheosis as the genuine Lich.

Just as quickly as one will denounce the Lich; claiming it a child of popular fiction, they will also criticize that the phylactery is an invention of modern fantasy. This in fact is proof of individual ignorance. The term phylactery originates with the Jewish people as an ancient artifact which carried scripture and was worn on the forearm and above the brow. It was believed that this simple leather box created a link to "God" whilst the devotee was in the depths of offering prayer. The definition of phylactery meant "to guard, protect" which is precisely what these did. Firstly, they protected the Torah scrolls and parchment that were placed within. Secondly, they created a shield of faith around the observant Jew who poured his heart and soul out, through the phylactery and out to his faulty god.

Much of the Cabal's magicks originated in Hungary, Slovakia, Germany, Saudi Arabia, and Syria. This is precisely where the Lich's phylactery came to be. In Damascus during the late 10900's HE, there was a group of clandestine necromancers who were observing the Jews and their operations with these *tefillin*, as they were known. It became strikingly clear that there was indeed a connection made with use and there occurred a natural exchange of energies between the spirit and their blind god, Yahweh. To this end, they sought to study this in more detail and note the full reason for this exchange as well as how to manipulate it.

In order to accomplish this mission, the necromancers commonly resorted to abduction and brutality to acquire a living subject which to observe and use extensive abuse to drive more desperation to the spiritual fore. In this manner, the necromancers could observe a greater exchange of energies the "closer to 'god'" the tortured subjects became. Those final moments right before death overtook them created the highest influx of spiritual energy and potential for transformation. In their experiments, they found that the more devoted Jews were able to withstand far more punishment and could survive when others of similar age and physical makeup would expire. This was of no particular surprise as the force of spirit was already well documented. However, this forged the hypothesis that genuine will, which is necessary for all successful rites combined with proper magicks could potentially create the very agent for absolute transfiguration.

Ensuing for centuries were a multitude of inhuman and savage ritual experiments focused on creating a permanent link which would deliver an exponentially stronger flow of spirit energy which would totally sustain the body. Unfortunately, these experiments only manifested awkward changes with the bodily form as well as hastened aging and death. The Syrian necromancers were already familiar with the ghouls that roamed about the deserts and mountains alike, but knowing they were already undead soon came to offer the final piece of the puzzle: undead augmentation. Necromancers and the undead have always carried a bizarre relationship where despite the typical lack of care for the living by the undead, necromancers had earned a special place beside them for their works, which facilitated the undertakings of each other. Therefore, the necromancers began experimenting with using both a blood offering of self as well as augmenting it with the ghouls'. This would prove to yield the first successful transfiguration.

By combining bloods into the phylactery, the necromancer was able to create a full transmogrification of self by pouring heart and soul into the phylactery which was now anchored to the ghoul. This then created another ghoul from the once mortal necromancer's flesh vessel. From this initial success, they realized that what they had missed was a supernatural anchor whereas the Jews had attempted to anchor their phylacteries to Yahweh. This anchor for the necromancers would be an undead being that already walked the realm or a Demon, Spirit, or a god or goddess of death. Because of this requisite anchor, there developed a great deal of communion between the necromancers and the entity they most wished to become akin to. Generations later, in the 11400's HE, the wife of the first Grandmaster, Syra would bring this knowledge to the Cabal, yet this would not complete the grand formulae by which the Cabal would use, as the Buried King, Zazazel and Patron of the Tower of Atrophy had his own method.

In life, his name was Brenhin. A Slovakian boy who had begun learning the magickal arts fled from home when his father had murdered his mother, a worker of the spirits of the fey lands. Brenhin learned from a sorceress who had in her own twisted way adopted the young man. What he did not realize was that she was merely grooming him to grow in such power that when he was ripe, she would consume his soul and extend her life. Through his own workings of divination with the Spirit known as Rishar, Brenhin realized that his end would come at the hand of his teacher. Therefore, before she could harm him, he instead killed her and through ritual vampirism, consumed her soul. Empowered, he sought a phylactery for himself, though at the time, he only knew that he required some type of relic which would safely house any residual or excess spiritual essence. Having happened upon an iron-covered skull, he thought to make that his personal device for the transference of spirit. Through his own experimentation, Brenhin learned that through self-inflicted brutalization and bloodletting, he could not only transfer this excess essence, but also transmute it into something more potent, maligned and eternal. He continued to speak with the Spirits who had accompanied him through his journeys until it was explained that he required an anchor. This anchor was of no particular deity or being, but rather an exceptionally powerful egregore of his own creation; a being which was a representation of himself in full apotheosis.

After years of ritual; bloodletting, soul-siphoning and expunging himself of ego and identity, Brenhin was able to fully take on a new flesh and spirit; the self in apotheosis: Zazazel. These long years in seclusion spent killing himself for an opportunity of harnessing an otherworldly power finally came and he would rise up a Lich in the flesh of a dead man. He held closely to the name given him in sinister whispers all of those years. In his triumph, the gate was opened to Maergzjirah and the Black God, Cernobog offered him a seat in the Eternal Grave as a Patron to necromancers and other death-obsessed disciples of the path of atrophy.

Syra was the first necromancer to be part of the Maergzjiran Cabal following the first Cabal Patriarch, Sybastien's blood pact with Cernobog. When she came to know the other Blighted Lords of Maergzjirah, she instantly became a servant of Zazazel. By combining her native method from her Syrian ancestors and the Buried King's, an entirely new form of transfiguration via phylactery was born. This entire formula consists of the following: a chosen vessel for the energies to be poured into and exchanged, an anchor, sacrifice of self via blood, spirit, life breath, etc., prayer and meditation, and most importantly, a properly aligned soul. Without possessing all of these

requisites, the necromancer is sure to destroy himself rather than ever achieve any glimpse of immortality for all he will do is poison his soul and self-destruct. In order to obtain Lichdom, you must push yourself to the threshold of death, but you cannot die. If you return to life, you have failed to transform, yet to die is to lose the battle for immortality. At the threshold you must transmogrify. It is in those final moments; as your body begins to fail and your identity is contained only by your phylactery bathing in a pool of blood can you be shrouded in undeath. For he who strives mightily and is of pure intent while devoting himself to the nightly bloodying and punishing of his flesh vessel will find that in the end, he is no longer mortal; no longer who he was a time ago, but rather immortalized and purified through undeath. The necromancer's pinnacle is in attaining immortality through undeath apotheosis. It is in this state that he no longer ages, requires no sustenance other than what he desires to ingest; time and physics are invalid to the Lich and nature is a laughable concept for there is nothing natural about him.

There is yet more as the rituals that prelude the magnum opus of Lich rites create a terrifying foundation for this unholy, undead fiend to emerge. Ages ago, this plane was a less guarded prison than it is today and therefore, magick was easier to manifest. Today, with technology, mental poisoning and the death grip of governments, societal regimes and religion, their oppressive and suppressive nature has created a thick filter over this realm which requires extreme action to manifest otherworldly results. Therefore, we must push further, harder and break the veil if we are to acquire such a grand treasure as immortality.

The phylactery is the catalyst for the Lich's transformation. However, it requires more. Aside from the mass blood sacrifices that the necromancer performs over the anchored heart of the phylactery, he seeks to deaden himself as much as possible. To this end, prior to taking up the last rites of the Lich, the necromancer undergoes what we refer to as the "Lich's

Wake". This is a time when the individual enters an extended seclusion among only the dead. This may be undertaken in a mausoleum, abandoned hospital or asylum, battlefield, or known areas that harbor expansive vortexes to the realm of the dead. Here, the necromancer will deprive himself of sustenance save for only necessary amounts of water, stale bread and expired offerings to the deceased. If possible, the necromancer should seek a level of intimacy with the dead, such as sleeping beside the corpses and using their bones for divination. This is deepened through corpse divination which animates the cadaver on a base level enough for speech, whereby the Spirits speak through the remains to reveal answers to the necromancer's inquiries. Offerings of life breath and blood are made throughout the day and night to the Spirits of Keraktes, the Eternal Grave and continuous chanting is performed to align the soul with the undead current. Typically speaking, most necromancers will remain in this seclusion for a month or more by which point there is little left of the individual. What comes next for the necromancer is a series of rites that tear apart the veil and allow the Spirits to begin their own preparation for the Lich hopeful.

Having deadened his flesh and soul; turning his mind only to his immortality through undeath, the necromancer now begins the Black Harvest. During this time, the necromancer seeks to successfully unleash two great evils into the world. The first is the Keraktian Sinkhole and the other is to execute the Innocent Sacrifice. These two rites concluded bring the necromancer to the threshold of Lichdom and only the final rite remains.

The Keraktian Sinkhole is a terrifying thing for in the midst of ritual, the necromancer is able to drive such a powerful spike of malevolent energy into the plane that there is now a tear in the planar fabric that cannot be closed. This open wound leaves the gate easily accessible for the undead to emerge forth and ravage this realm. Further, one can watch as the world around the sinkhole begins to die off. Vegetation and animal life is snuffed out and mortality rates spike. The intent of bringing death becomes a personal agenda amongst the mundane who adhere to their high morals and therefore, one may watch as they tear apart one another like rabid animals for no reason other than to spread the influence of death in their madness. With time, the sinkhole grows and its influence over all life is expanded in kind. This creates a powerful vortex that spews forth the raw death essence required by the necromancer for his work to be complete.

As said, there is another ritual; one of culling set forth by the Lady Nhilmice, Patroness in Keraktes and Watcher of the Gate of the Eternal Grave, translated from her native tongue as "The Innocent Sacrifice", which is another matter that is kept well only to the necromancer as it requires the total sacrifice of an innocent. This is not referencing the morally innocent or weak, youthful children. This simply is a mocking tone to represent anyone who does not bend a knee to the ways of the dark path. The enemy. I am quite sure that everyone who reads this has someone in mind that they would delight in the opportunity to lay upon their sacrificial altar and rip their mind and soul out and carve their flesh; brutalizing every last aspect of their being until nothing remained, but a vile display of horrid intentions. While physical sacrifice is technically not required, as hexes, soulrape and binding can accomplish similar results, it tends to push the individual completely beyond a point of no return. It is total liberation of self.

The Last Rite of the Lich represents the final ritual the necromancer will perform to achieve his apotheosis via undeath. This requires the necromancer to be steadied in his personal ritual space that is now a wide open gateway to the Eternal Grave; a sub-plane of death. With a special elixir, incense and his phylactery, he will cast away any aspect of his mortality that remains; shedding life, identity and the world he knew in an effort to bury any semblance of his former self to be reborn a Lich. It should be noted that even now, even in these final moments when triumph seems automatic, if the necromancer retains any desire to remain or has not fulfilled his proper requirements for apotheosis, this rite will become toxic and he will surely die in a very negative and unproductive way. Lichdom will be forever lost and all that he has worked for will be just a faded memory. However, should one be so devoted to their path of Lichdom and rightly obtain that state, he can truly rest his bones beside the gods of darkness and death. The Lich is otherworldly, unnatural; supernatural. This undead necromancer possesses terrifying power and a constant flow of death essence, for death now obeys his eternal will. Thoughts are mere extensions of deeper self and therefore manifest in their desired form instantly. One's touch is lethal and their blood is a sacred libation in and of itself. Truly, nothing can kill the Lich and should his physical body be destroyed by some atomic degree of carnage, the phylactery retains his spirit which is then given free rein to find and possess a new body. As an immortal being, the possibilities for this world are endless, yet now the gates to other worlds open for nothing can actively hold the Lich.

For some, the Lich is a commendable, but unattainable concept. For others it is a nightmare they serve while others see the Lich as an unholy creature they wish only to escape. In the Cabal, the Lich is something we seek to become absolutely when we walk the path of atrophy. We have the Buried King, Zazazel to look to for guidance and inspiration and we have a cadre of Spirits in Keraktes, the Eternal Grave to assist us in our discoveries and execution. We Cabal Necromancers have our Maergzjiran ancestors who have achieved apotheosis and left behind their path notes. Lichdom is not something distant, nor is it merely a state of mind. It is absolute. Immortality. It is eternal undeath and uncontested power surging forth from Keraktes through our hands, crackling like black fire and cascading lightning.

Like all other disciples of the path of death, I know you desire unparalleled power and eternity to be firmly nestled in your hands. It can only be achieved through apotheosis. However, it cannot be grasped unless you are willing to die by your own hand through the brutal, torturous, methodical and bloody rites of the Lich; anchored to a realm of cold, darkness and despair. While you sit and weigh your stance and options, hoping to gain some advantage through shortcuts and to avoid the inevitable, you must know that eternity awaits, but only for those who throw themselves into the maw of the grave with complete abandon. It is only when you can openly accept your doom and invite death can you possess the final key to apotheosis. The key to Lichdom rests within the lock on the gate to undeath. Push yourself to the threshold and there you shall find it waiting for you to unlock the gate and step forth an undead master of the soul; a living embodiment of fear, defiance and death. You return from the threshold a Lich.

▪ Somnus Dreadwood

Ascended Grandmaster of the Maergzjiran Cabal, Master of Atrophy

THE NATURE OF BRAZILIAN QUIMBANDA
Danilo Coppini[1]

---

[1] Translation courtesy of Soror Carolina Malvezi & Fr Shadow.

The true nature and essence of Brazilian Quimbanda has remained in obscurity for a long time because this is a Tradition which transmits knowledge through *direct training* and has in truth been unveiled to only a few adepts. Many of these adepts abandoned the "Path of Maioral" because they could not withstand the heat and pressure intrinsic to the process of internal alchemy within this current. Those few who pushed forward, shaped their own private lineages in Quimbanda according their personal gnosis and development, therefore there are several forms by which the cult is practiced in Brazil.

Regardless of what form each lineage or line of practice has taken, one cannot ignore the source elements of tradition and the importance of personal training of the *Zelador* (What we call "zelador" is essentially a Priest of the Cult- one who serves the Exus and oversees the spiritual development of the adepts within their circle); Quimbanda has specific elements which should be taken into consideration by those who feel called to walk this path. The nature of real Quimbanda, unlike other religions and cults, is not concerned with development of a moral conduct or refined ethic and is in no way geared toward the values or interests of humanity society. As well, it is not a way in which adepts will feel spiritual satisfaction for a whilst dwelling in the material body, the aim of Quimbanda is not to manifest satisfaction and it has as it's objective ruthless liberation, because "satisfaction" in the material dimensions of the Demiurge is illusion.

Brazilian Quimbanda actually even delves into correlation of the conscious and unconscious. It is the arduous way that has as it's goal genuine self-knowledge and, quite pronouncedly, the knowledge of one's role in this life and in relation betwixt one's self and current system to master the balance of the physical, astral and spiritual bodies with the evolutionary (or slavery) path that the initiate will choose.

"Feelings" are mechanisms must be cultivated or corrected for all adepts of Quimbanda. We understand that each adept as an individual person (and all adepts collectively) are free to ascertain their own self parameters with no imposition about what is "Good or Evil". What is interesting here is that certain Exus have revealed to us that there exist unseen energetic shackles which bind us to positive and negative values, because do not undertsand why we feel the way we do about everything. This lack of awareness holds us in invisible webs in which the wires of "morality" suffocate the spirit. If feelings are inevitable, they must be cultivated and employed to stimulate multiple visions and capacities with discernment and higher aims, discarding the concepts of morality and ethics so subserviently accepted by the mindless obediant masses. Exu is the seed that breaks the earth and gives life; not a tree that is born with fruit.

This process of self-knowledge aims to dominate and understand feelings and emotions to create tangible thoughts projecting intent as a more method to have communication with the spiritual world. To achieve this the adept must experience various situations, and deeper experiences – sometimes painful. Until the adept understands that everything in them emanated and felt shapes in their journey, and that the mind is mediator between self and path of one's Exu, they will wander through subjective interpretation and sometimes face many difficulties. Quimbanda does not want perfect adepts, but wants unbound and liberated sparks of Chaos- minds which transcend limiting forms and go beyond moral and ethical concepts.

QUIMBANDA & PREDATORY INSTINCTS

The awakened man was blessed by the Illumination of Quimbanda. It is one of the rays of Lucifer, working in an internal war against chains of the Cyclic Slavery System (reincarnations and Karma). To shatter the limitations of these obstacles, the spirit must be fed often by the source of wisdom and, at the same time, the instincts of a predator must be developed. Wisdom does not counteract predatory action, it gives the adept the discernment to know when, how and the intensity of ferocity which should be triggered. It is not to restrict, but to adapt our instincts to the reality that we live in an environment which is hostile toward Satanic Becoming.

The adepts create in their self an aversion of weakness and social limitations. Predators do not cry for their prey, nor do they spend energy on an unfruitful hunt. Real predators rarely make mistakes because they are guided by wisdom and instinct attained through self-knowledge. The advanced adept knows his own limits and limitations.

Humans are conditioned to the instinct of self-preservation. They fight unceasingly for life and their beleifs. This mechanism is regulated by *pain* and *fear*, that is, they remain alive because these two act as stimulants. Fear releases adrenaline which increases physical strength and heightens the senses as observed in soldiers about to face combat. The adepts of Quimbanda learn to embrace or sense a battle not as a decision motivated by feelings or sensations, but yes, by the cold predatory instinct, strong and incisive. They are not hostages of their own fear, neither of pain, because they understand their own nature and the nature of the spirits which teach them.

Exus are spirits with the capacity to walk in a timeless line (past, present and future). Because Exus and Pomba Giras (pronounced *Pombah-Jeerah*) often watch their children from the astral plane, the time line is not restricted only to the current incarnation wherein our consciousness currently moves. These spirits can walk in our previous lives and modify, in a beneificial way, our present life. So, Exu can cause phobias of previous lives in this live as an instinctual boundary against destructive tendencies. Without deepening on the subject, they also stimulate such impulses to make stronger the predatory instincts as they awaken within initiates.

FIRE SPIRIT X WATER SPIRIT

The world we live in, cyclic and rotary, produces perceptible and imperceptible changes all the time. We understand this world as the "captivity" wherein different kinds of souls are in the raw/ solidified/ material state. Every change of the world provides change in its flock, that is, even major changes discrete as they may be, bear effect on humans. The rhythm of these changes can be variable and reach the collective as well as the individual in different stages forcing all living into a necessary adaptation process.

Obviously there exist theories concerning human behavior the evolution process however in our cult, we emphasize two elements: Will and Desire. Through these impulses outcrops an attitude of ostracism and dynamism in certain individual's behavioral patterns. This is divided in various stages, however we wish to contrast two specific qualities: Furious and Meek.

The furious behavior is endowed with Fire-evolution, and aggression and the need to always overcome and climb higher. This enables the human to see the changes of the world, its consequences and creates a multiplicity of actions possible to enact with these changes. People with furious behavior quickly grasp and master external action and possess a certain ambience able to create stability in uncertain situations, ceasing to be a tool wich cooperates with the System. People with this behavior can learn quickly from their mistakes and although mature and gentlemanly are not easily contained or controlled. They never cease to breaking boundaries, desires, frustrations and aspirations in both systems and organizations.

Meek behavior is like sitting water preferring safety, stability and protection against the aggressive currents of nature. Usually this breed of individual creates their identity based on profane materialistic and superficial pleasures which essentially profile the sum of their aspirations. They have fear on many levels and usually heavy social-anxiety. They dwell on their traumas and loss, making new obstacles to block changes. They cannot support a competitive and innovative environment and they have linear habits and difficulty with innovative changes. These weak slaves best serve positions of obediance.

Both behaviors coexist in society and they have family, friends, and dreams. They face the same problems, crises and all complexity of this system. They compete for the same space and they are susceptible to changes in the world. The person with furious behavior and the person with meek behavior can, in a moment, be closer to the Cult of Exu. The reasons that lead to such decisions may be the same because are not all person who looks for this cult to have spiritual development and evolution, whether furious or meek. Inside of the cult both will live the same stages and in this point they differ.

Now, imagine Exu interfering aggressively in the time line of these people, with different behaviors (furious or meek). The aggressiveness will empower significant changes in their material lives but at the same time will create confusion and hard ways until they secure road for themselves, or a "new way".

A person with furious behavior will surely support this confusion because they can quickly adapt and will see thought the "spaces" left by their Exu. This person will make the most of this opportunity and will not allow the frustrations to interfere because built they possess faith with subjectivity. So this person will regenerate in the sacred forms that Spirits emit and not trough the forms that coarse feelings try to create.

A person with meek behavior will likely collapse seeing the protector structure falling. This person will cry for not having listened to the teachings of the Red and Black Flame and will allow traumas to dominate their lives. This person will not support the opening of new ways and will break into coarse pieces.

Exu, in his infinite wisdom and with his hellish laugh which banishes, will pass between watching both two people with different behaviors. The person with furious behavior will fall into the abyss becoming a vessel able to promote the resurrection of dark ancestors, so the person with meek behavior will broken into coarse pieces until Exu casts them abroad because they are not aligned to his chaos.

This work demonstrates how many people who pursue the path of Exu leave the path and became enemies of this power. They are passive, inert and hope changes coming in a linear way, calm and protectionist. These people usually hide in different religious way that spread subtlety, love, compassion and benevolence. They think their Exu will just plant a "tree of money" or "send them a lover in three days" because these situations cooperate with their lethargic and anti-evolutionist stages and need for the warmth of affluent lifestyles.

Remember Exu is a force of constant motion and will never will stagnate. "Exu does not give the fish for who does not know how to fish!" Exu teach us how to act as catalysts!

Ego is the defense mechanism of the personality, structure of psychic system that leads us to reality. The ego is the "advocate of fear" and restrains every predatory instinct that we have.

Identify your own predatory instincts and do not restrain them. Restraint means to repress, express denial. To see is to accept and to understand the impulse to the same which must be awakened when needed. Restraint generates dissatisfaction, loss and weakness. These feelings, in this context, attract Karma which acts as cuffs for the Slavery System of the False God. Understanding your own impulses is part of Liberation and the self-knowledge.

THE LION´S ROAR:
THE BHAKTI PRATICE IN THE SINISTER WAY
AShTarot Cognatus

WHO IS LORD NRSIMHADEVA?

According with the Vedic scripture Srimad Bhagavatam, Lord Nrsimhadeva is an avatar (incarnation) of Krishna, that came to kill the asura (demon) Hiranyakashpur and protect his devotee Prahlada Maharaj. Hiranyakashpur is the father of Prahlada Maharaj and did not like that his son would realize devotional pratices, so he engaged his servants such as Sukracharya to teach diplomacy and other philosophies to deviate Prahlada from the devotional path.

Hiranyakashpur did several austerities and asked a blessing from Lord Brahma so that he could be immortal, but Brahma could not bestow this because he himself is not imortal, though he has a long span of life. In this way, Brahma bestowed the blessing that Hiranyakashpur could not be killed at daytime, not at night time; not inside, not outside a house; not killed by man, not by animal; not by weapon, not by someone's hands; not on earth, not in sky.

One time, Hriranyakashpur was asking Prahlada Maharaj, where it would be this Supreme Lord that he worshipped so much, Prahlada, being a jnana-bhakta[2], replied that the Lord resided everywhere. Hriranyakashpur in a rage asked then, "Would he be in this pillar?"

and struck the pillar from inside which came Lord Nrsimhadeva, a half-man half-lion form. There was then a long fight between Lord Nrsimhadeva and Hiranyakashpur until sunset, when Nrisimhadeva takes Hiranyakashpur onto his lap and opens his stomach with his sharp nails, creating a garland with the entrails of his intestines.

In this way we can notice that the way that Nrisimhadeva kills Hiranyakashpur respects the blessings of Lord Brahma, killing him not at daytime, not at nighttime, but in the dusk. Not inside, not outside the house but on the veranda. Not by man, not by animal but by a mix of both. Not by weapon, nor by the hands of someone but by the fangs of Nrisimhadeva. Not on the earth, not in the sky instead in the very lap of Nrisimhadeva.

NRSIMHADEVA DRINKS THE BLOOD OF HIRANYAKASHPUR

It is said in some Puranas that Nrisimhadeva drinks all the blood of Hiranyakashpur. We can notice then that Nrisimhadeva is linked to vampirism. Emperor Norduk of the vampiric group Tempel of Azagthoth, describes in which way Nrisimhadeva is linked to vampirism in his text *Teachings of Narayana: Vampirism Revelead within Vaisnavism*. In this text we see that Nrisimhadeva, being a form of Krishna, represents the Shadow Being aspect in his angry form (Ugra-Nrisimha). This angry aspect of Krishna comes to defeat ignorance, represented as Hiranyakashpur and other asuras (demons). The asuras always try to prevent the development of the adepts and because of this they need to be strongly annihilated so there will be progress. Emperor Norduk says also that demons are ignorant people and that those who

---

[2] Bhakti-yoga is the union with the divinity through devotion. The practice (sadhana) involves the singing of mantras, devotional songs, deity worship in the altar and other methods. Jnana-yoga is the union with divinity in his impersonal aspect (Brahman) through selfknowledge (Jnana/Gnosis). Its practices involves contemplation of being (atman) in unity with Brahman. Jnana-misra-bhakti is the mixed (misra) practice of jnana and bhakti, where the jnana-bhakta see his deity present at all things, as Pralada Maharaj replied to his father.

ignore the Vedic wisdom, that is, the common people of everyday life.

Thus, as Nrisimhadeva drinks the blood of Hiranyakashpur, the vampiric adept drains the vital energy of his victims and offers his chalice of blood to Narayana Vampire (a form of Krishna as the Supersoul, residing in the heart). This will be retransmitted to the adepts in the form of "Rain of Mercy" of vampiric teaching and will be as prasada (offered food) to Krishna. This consists in a form of alchemy, that the adept devotee seek to feed only of prasada, and this will cause a transformation of consciouness, entering in communion with his deity by mystery of eucharist.

BHAKTI AND THE BLACK FLAME

The black flame is the essence of the adept that shines at his heart. To practice bhakti is to expand this black flame from the heart and to see the divinity worshipped arise in the middle of it, just as Nrsimhadeva arises from the middle of pillar.

There are many practices to honor Nrisimhadeva that we can learn from a experienced person on it or that possess a real spiritual realization. To this person that possess realization is to whom we give the name guru (spiritual master), one that one that removes (ru) the darkness (gu) from ignorance with the torch of spiritual knowledge. This can be seen as linked to the Luciferian symbolism, where Lucifer is the bringer of light (lux-light, ferrebearer) and brings together with his fallen angels knowledge to the human carriers of the witch-blood.

The guru then initiates the disciples in practices such as the nrsimha-mantra, the chanting of maha-mantra and other mantras to expand the black flame of the disciple through the bhakti-yoga practice, also known as sadhana-bhakti. Some mantras such as the nrsimha-mantra and other diksha-mantras, such as the gopala-mantra, kama-gayatri, etc. need to be received through the ceremony of diksha (initiation).

Others can be freely chanted like the Hare Krishna maha-mantra (Hare Krishna Hare Krishna Krishna Krishna Hare Hare Hare Rama Hare Rama Rama Rama Hare Hare) as well as diverse devotional songs. From the songs that can be chanted to Nrsimhadeva, we highlight a portion of one of them below:

namas te narasimhāya prahlādāhlāda-dāyine hiraṇyakaśipor vakṣaḥ- śilā- ṭaṅka-nakhālaye

ito nṛsimhaḥ parato nṛsimho yato yato yāmi tato nṛsimhaḥ bahir nṛsimho hṛdaye nṛsimho nṛsimham ādiṁ śaraṇaṁ prapadye

tava kara-kamala-vare nakham adbhuta-śṛngaṁ dalita-hiraṇyakaśipu-tanu-bhṛngam keśava dhṛta-narahari-rūpa jaya jagadīśa hare

TRANSLATION

"I offer my obeisances to Lord Narasimha, who gives joy to Prahlada Maharaja and whose nails are like chisels on the stone like chest of the demon Hiranyakasipu.

Lord Nrsimha is here and also there. Wherever I go Lord Nrsimha is there. He is in the heart and is outside as well. I surrender to Lord Nrsimha, the origin of all things and the supreme refuge.

O Kesava! O Lord of the universe! O Lord Hari, who have assumed the form of half-man, halflionl All glories to You! Just as one can easily crush a wasp between one's fingernails, so in the same way the body of the wasp like demon Hiranyakasipu has been ripped apart by the wonderful pointed nails on Your beautiful lotus hands."

SINISTER ALTAR

Those that want to worship Nrisimhadeva can also create an altar with His image and always offer flowers, incense and lacto-vegetarian foods in front of His image. With the execution of these devotional acts, gradually the adept shall be feeling his own black flame expanding, with Nrisimhadeva inside his heart bringing strenghth and protecting him from the obstacles of the sinister path.

Jay Nrisimhadev Bhagavan!

VLF Laboratories

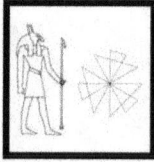

Q.309

GNOSIS AND ACTION

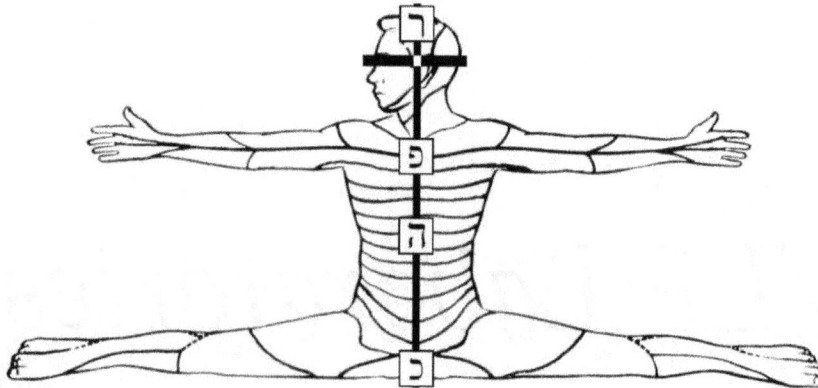

Ayin-me-Yesh

–

A brief introduction to the Q.309 system (ver 0.1)

April 2016

The acronym Q.309 indicates a system that studies, experiments and uses a Gnostic-ecstatic method, characterized by a noetic model, to stimulate and convey a change in the phenomenal perception of human existence.

Q.309 has its action field for its Opus Luxuriae in the Matter and in the energy that Matter conveys.

Q.309 is the setian push to the permanent change in function of an indeterminate and undifferentiated ideal tending towards a dimensionless entropic un-reality.

Q.309 makes its first reductio ad unum not acknowledging any practical difference between sacred acts and mundane acts, using effectively every resource at its disposal to attract the triad time-matter-space to an anthropocentric dimension.

Q.309 enhances the square as the flesh's diagram with the coordinates Ʋ and U, where Ʋ is the material fire and U is the use of the energy accumulated through ꓸ the not-thinking light active in Assiah.

These two glyphs create in their interaction the name-action that determines the current 309: Set as "the one who created himself", transcending the original cosmic egg allegory and canceling the concepts of "cyclical", "renewal" and "rebirth".

Set, channeled in the current 309 in all its aspects, allows the creation of thought/action to influence Assiah to a Setian nature of perpetual turbulence.

This transmutation of perceptions takes place on a practical level through the left eye of Set, the physical mode of the anti-pathway 26, which is renewing intelligence directly in contact with the

genital apparatus, the Via Venerea, that uses
Matter as a vehicle for fulfillment.

Q.309 requires a union to the divine sphere
through an *imitatio dei*.

This Saturnian paradox is the setian axis mundi
that combines all existential and perceptual
frequencies and connects Pulse, Abstraction,
Construction and Action with their antithesis
represented by the system of the Four Absences of
the 'Matter of Wish' to an experience of permanent
Ek-stasis.

Q.309 argues that the divine is a mechanical
process activated by the actions.

The Logos of our strategy is summarized in the
Modulation of K.H.P.R.

K.H.P.R. is the vocalization of Set in Heh (Set
from the infinite future) that acts to redefine
the subject-object interface resizing the
antagonistic impulse between the two.

K: No Space
H: No Matter
P: No Existence
R: No Light

The proper implementation of this concepts leads
to the last phase of the Setian experience, the
annulment of thought, the ecstatic union,
ontological and epistemic, of the human sphere
with the Singularity.

The formula KHPR has connections with every
practical act of Q.309 system.

The manifest universe is a constant transformation
of energy into matter and vice versa.
The body is connected to this action where the
matter, if inert, is the limit and denial and
produces a distorted perception of the energy
dissipated in the creation of the illusion
commonly called reality.
Setian strategy to disengage from this cyclical
situation is to reverse the path of creation

retracing the trail from the manifest matter to
the un-manifest unum through the phases of
degeneration of coagulants systems of what is
created. reversing them.
The goal is not the mystical experience itself,
but the use of the latter in order to unite
thought and reality, to intervene actively in the
existential frequencies dragging the light of
other phenomenal spheres in this dimension.
The cancellation of thought is preceded by the
union in the singularity.

This manifest correlation between Thought/action
and divine presence makes it possible that, with
adequate measures, you can 'drag' down the
potentials of higher frequencies that manifest
reality and facilitate their permanence freeing
the setian flow from the concept of NM-N-STS
(skin/concealment): inert materiality.

The Thought represents the dynamism in Assiah, it
does not need to be translated into action on the
material plane to activate its potential: it is
already in action when it is formulated.

Q.309 summarizes in two coordinates its modus
operandi:

1 - the tendency to a-causality: the interruption
of Thought in its cause-effect coordinates and
intentionality in its use on the materiality.

2 - the awareness of being involved in the
dissociation from cosmic events and, accordingly,
the structuring of the Thought/action in a non-
dimensional scenario.

Q.309 so cancels the laws of karma and denies the
balance as the ultimate goal, being Q.309 a mean
towards a form of active, dynamic and constantly
evolving eternity.

Q.309 has, as its ultimate goal, the chaos that is
the reduction of sensory experience to a formless
and timeless point that transcends the rules of
stasis and cyclicality, necessary for the
maintenance of matter, opposing the antithesis of

what is formed, limited, causal, orderly to this
eternal return.

The constant development is the way of Setian
chaos which starts from ego, perceptual/cognitive
element formed on the experience of cosmic
existence limitations, and ends with the
consciousness of the self, which is the latent
inner force of chaos and is used as an ideal
connection with the motion of tehom, the abyss
that secretes the chaos, when properly activated.

Q.309 is, to end this introduction, a way to break
up the processes of the linear causality by
mutating them, through the consciousness and
perception, to a more profound and effective
meaning.

Q.309 deprecates the simplistic use of the
symbolic, traditionally understood as a key to
describe the reality.

O = 1/2 = 11
We are the Sitra Achra

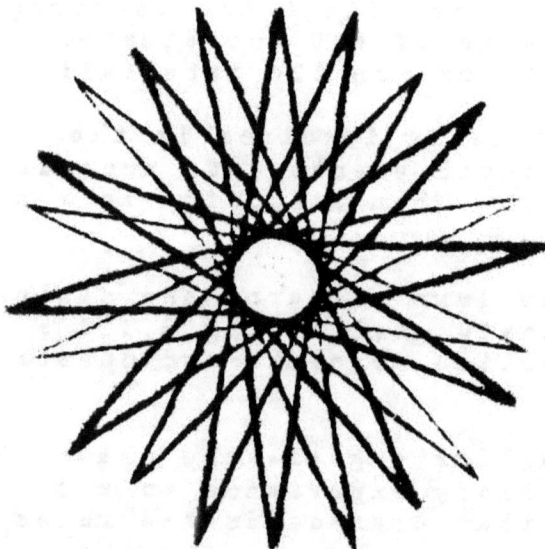

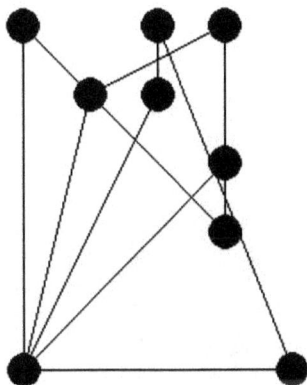

Q.309 promote the Perpetual Gnostic turbulence

All © by Q.309 / Rev. A.Ra'Ah
www.q309.wordpress.com

appendix A

We celebrate the Flesh
against the lies
of the spirit

appendix B

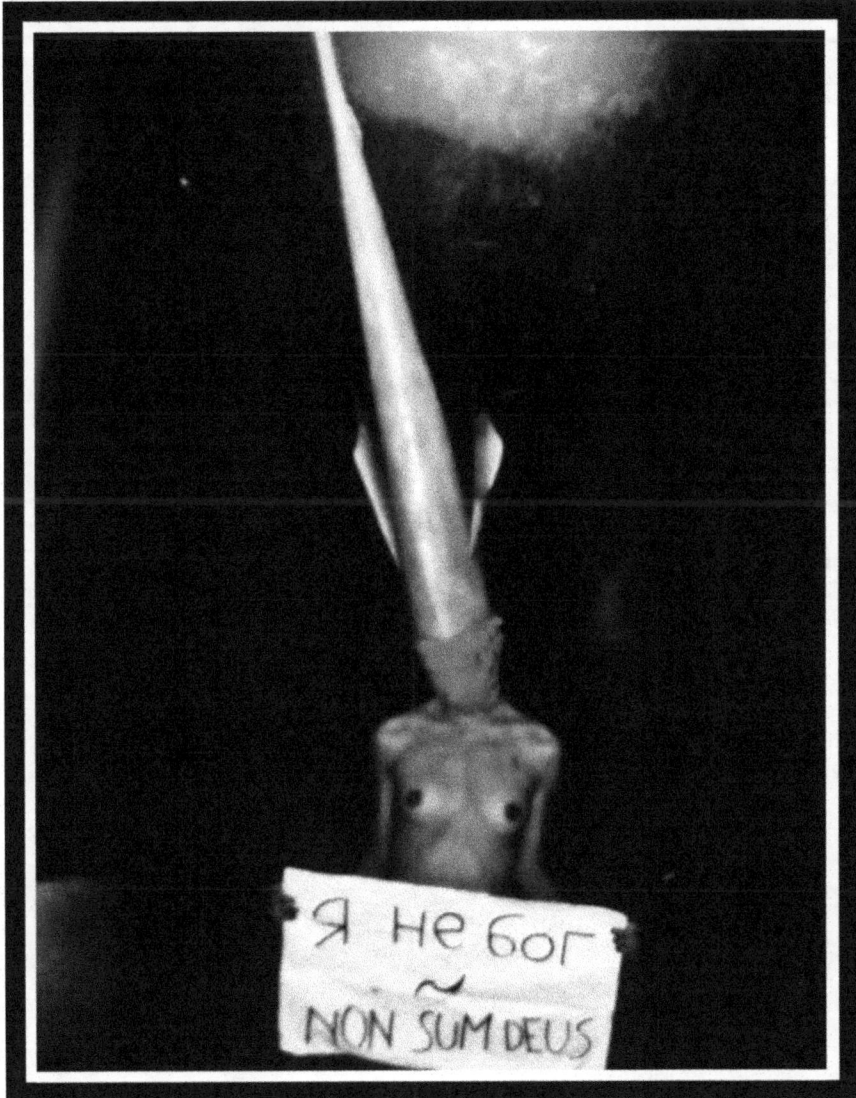

WE destroy your symbols
WE destroy you

Crude Azathoth

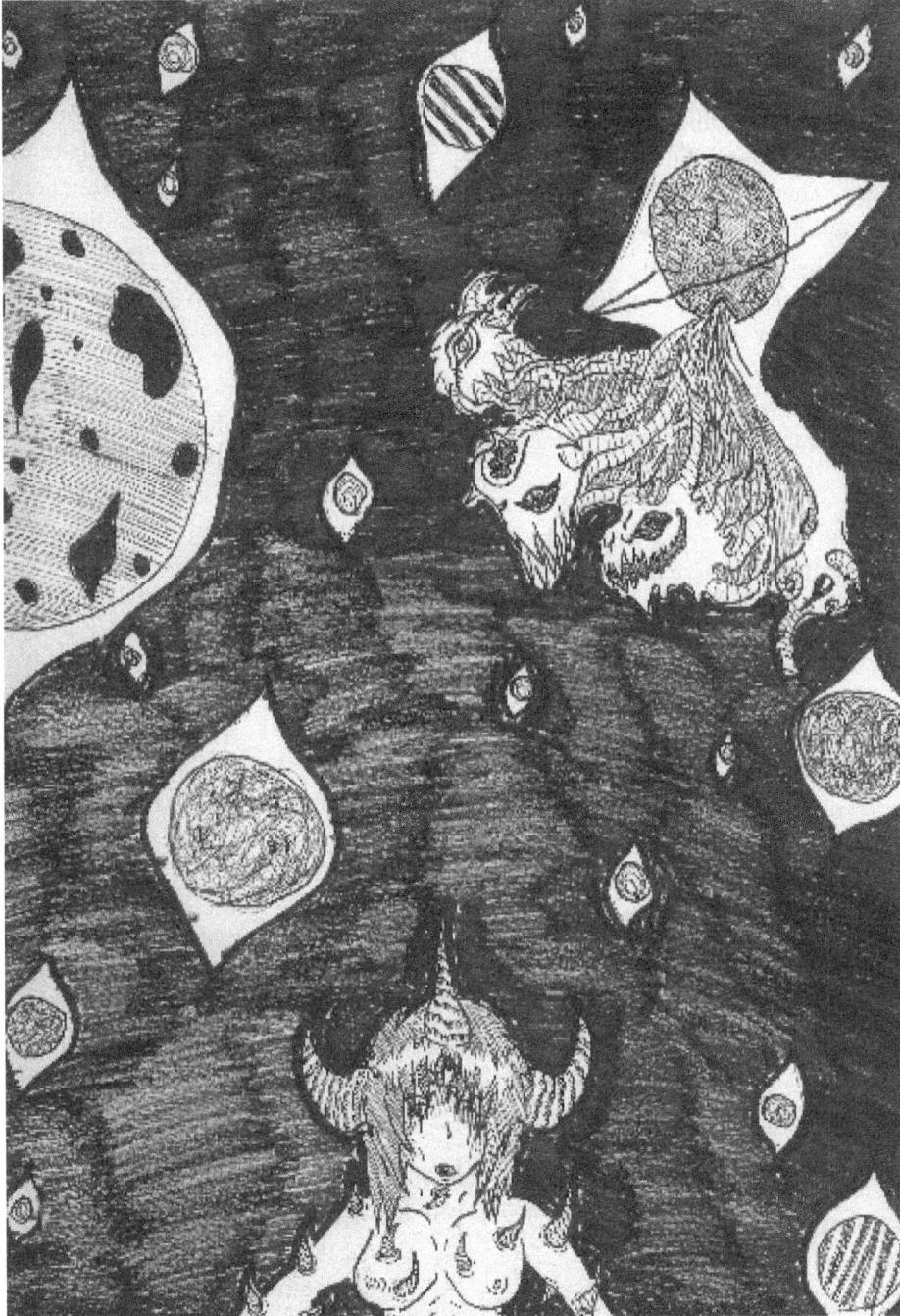

THE ASTRAL TERRORS OF 'THE BLACK DEVILS'

Whilst working with 'The Black Devils', the innate must acquire a high, spiritually, Shaitānic vibrancy; if one is lacking in this area, the initiate will undergo a probation, or psychic observation from a nonhuman entity (Jinn), for the course of 49 days. This Shaitānic vibrancy (shared amongst 'The Black Devils') attracts THEM, and allows the sorcerer to commune/befriend THEM. Jinn originally translates to the 'hidden' or 'concealed' ones. When Allah's blasphemy lighted this cosmos, the angels pushed, and forced down our darkest, infernal family (Including Azazel) into the shadows, and cracks of the unseen at Mt. Hermon...

They still dream & savagely twist, and turn as the aeons pass, awaiting the arrival of the great Ad Dajjal, to tear with tooth, and claw at the threshold of our reality.

We fell out of touch with our infernal family nearly 2,000 years ago (in the birthing of the "White Lodge", which is now dying). Shaytans/Jinn (especially those of our father Azazel) can cause hellish nightmares (in which the initiate/ 'Black Devil' realizes darker aspects of their spiritual makeup that previously went unknown to conscious realization) sleep paralysis, insanity, ultraterrestrial visitation, and can also enhance our spiritually driven predatory/vampiric naturæ.

Their grip, and power must overwhelm the psychological, and input stimuli of the spiritual Jihadist. This allows the Wahsh (spiritual beast) to travel in between cracks of the mind & spirit, to seethe forth blood essence into the void.

We travel, worlds upon worlds, cursing & uttering chants of the universes demise, and inevitable return to the great abyss...

Over a progressive amount of time these direct spiritual confrontations leave an imprint, or stain upon the Ruh (false ego).

The intention of this imprint is to shock the spirit; overtime this allows us to commune with THEM, and thus can they transfer their spiritual fire via sacrifice, and bloodlet.... other means of communicating with THEM is through Salat (prayer), meditation, and certain breathing techniques, such as Pranayama.

Frenzied, and sporadic channels of demonically induced, hypnotic states comes unexpectedly, and often without warning. Leaving the 'Black Devil' to wander in utter confusion between the realms of the casual and acausal

Those who pledge allegiance to the infernal, and fiery realm of the 'Black City' will be spiritually tortured, terrified, and deeply (spiritually) wounded; this is for the advancement of attuning to a more choicest spiritual Wahsh, something beyond human comprehension, and rational...

The chosen of Azazel hear our Fathers great call, and know in their hearts how to gain the 'Secret of Secrets' (the spiritual fire of the adversary) from Sidi Azazel. Troops & magickians of 'The Black Devils'; spiritual soldiers, and shamans (not all are inclined to physically "fight", but should take the necessary precautions to know your next proverbial "move", to further the kingdoms manifestation physically; for instance, one can psychically/spiritually drain a subject/vessel without ever having come into physical contact with it. That is not to say that we denote real acts of physical evil, and chaos which will be provided by more clandestine, and natural deformations of the spirit, transmitted telepathically to each initiate.)

We are more focused upon the death of the

spirit, through direct confrontation with the nameless entities of the abyss)

Allow the flame of the Jinn to rest within the "clay" vessels of our mortal bodies, slowly melting away our spirit; harshly, and brutally transforming us into true devils!

This trait of 'The Black Devil' allows us to rape the accursed mundanity, that is the western ethos. We blaspheme The Blind One, the true deceiver!

Allah has kept us shackled in chains of orthodoxy, and societal indoctrination/ enslavement for millennia; this 'state of stagnation' (which will give rise to 'The Black Devils', as an antidote to the spiritual filth that now riddles this planet) has held us humans in a psychic, spiritual, and physical prison for the last 2,000 plus years...

Yet through THEM (our infernal family) we become FIRE, and thus transgress, go without, and Journey Beyond the influence of the Blind One (Allah, and his false light, consorts/angels) ...

The Jinn are Closer to the Shaytani, and all manner of living 'devils'. We must open that door between us, and THEM; opening up to the 'outside' is very dangerous, and fraught with terror, and trauma.

Those of 'The Black Devils' fully allow THEM to awaken the innermost shadows of their subconscious, and inevitably become possessed; to share a body with another entity of the abyss. To walk as a demon in the flesh!

We expose ourselves to filth, rot, and decay, that the spirit might die; that we may communicate with the (Wahsh) & go beyond the limitations of The Blind One, and his false light..

Darkness allows us to rip a hole in the universe & piece together the whole puzzle, all the way back to the absolute (Haawiya) within & without!

The programmed limitations of the "self" (a horrendous ploy of Allah) given to us by modern, and mediocre filters of deceit, have dumbed us down to such a base level, it appears absurd to the animating force of the cosmos. 'The Black Devil' should never be of a singular, spiritual, denotative identity. It's more akin to a hive mind resonate within the abyss herself!

When one pledges their mind, heart, body, and soul to Shaitān they become one with the collective hive mind of Haawiya, or "the spiritual cell" dedicated to bringing down the higher vibrations ov Hell & Chaos. 'The Eternal, Black City' awaits your response.

If there's one 'issue' I can stress the most, it's that of the "revolt"; which must first arise from within, you have to revolt against the spiritually imposed trash, and programmed response that have indoctrinated you into slavery since you were born, this must be spiritually realized in order to cause any real change in the realm of the spirit..

By this extended spiritual connexion to the Shaitānic current, 'The Black City' manifests itself in dreams and visions, that one day will come to fruition and commingle with 3D manifestation, meaning the LITERAL 'Black City' will become fully manifest upon this mud ball.

We will be able to become that fire which they (THEM) emanate! The eternal, Shaitānic flame, which comes directly through Sidi Azazel, our father and teacher!

Azazel lies in the chambers of forgetfulness, and is sought/seen & felt in times of spiritual crisis, this is why us, 'The Black Devils' must take that first step into the absolute and throw our shackles aside, allowing the darkness to breath into us!

Ya Umm Haawiya! Ya Ataghut!

Ya Al Fawdaa (O, the chaos!) springing forth from the waters of Umm Haawiya, enlivening the chosen of Shaitān! The gates between the stars, and our insatiable hearts, thirst for connection, that we might allow the children of our Lord within the inner sanctums of our spirit, and mind!

We must dream awake, and hear their call at the end of time...

'The Black Devils' are all comprised of the same source, our eternal mother, Umm Haawiya... however, we are locked away in this meat machine by a jealous and vindictive "God" who wants us to suffer, for he created this universe outside of the absolute.

'The Black Devils' willingly accept death & indeed tend to become close friends with the abyss, in which dreams and nightmares are made manifest within the conscious fiber of our physical being.

We need to fuel/feel their icy breath blown across our bones! Many practices can induce such states of possession and communion with THEM. Practice Dhikr, listen to heavy, industrial music, see yourself marching at the coming of the gates, see yourself in the black city; induce traumatic psychic interference..... Stay awake for days on end, ingest psychedelic compounds, shed blood, subject the body to extreme pain, etc...

The gift of spiritual sight is given to us through realization of the Wahsh (beast), and it's tremendous power fueled by Sidi Azazel. This allows insight of the eternal darkness, to remain in the rubble/dirt of the common place 'world'.... This is where visions, and dreams lie, in the true mud, and grime of life... Hide behind that rubble, let it suffocate you... Become one with that which the world has forgotten...

We're here, but for a short time, and will remain blind until we come to rest with our Father in infinite blackness...

Thrust yourself into the abyss & feel the eternal, and cleansing fires of Jahannam embrace you!

YA FA'UMMU'HU HAAWIYA

THE LEGION OF DEVILS
WITH ABSOLUTE SOULS
www.facebook.com/groups/TheBlackDevils333/

COATLICUE

VLF Laboratories: "Everything is connected through Flesh. In a universe of nothingness, you are your body." Q309

The epitome of raw unharnessed subversive hardcore, extreme dysfunctional porn and Kali Yuga eroticism. Transcending the flesh by means of releasing one's self of taboos, embracing depravity, perversity, debauchery, blasphemy and all it encompasses for we are of 'The Otherside', the Sitra Ahra. Marco's eye for directing, photography surpasses the senses enabling the viewer to be fully absorbed into an illicit aesthetic world of sexual gnosis unlike any other.

$$0 = \wedge / 2 = \wedge \wedge$$

As an avid fan/supporter in tribute and appreciation to the hard works of VLF Laboratories and his sultry crew with deep respect and adoration in which Marco Malattia has been a huge Inspiration, a highly intellectual beloved friend and much more, whom with great pleasure will be an honor working together in the near future to share in Maestro Malattia's vision.

Hail The God of Sexual Gnosis!

Hail Q309!

Coatlicue

THE SATURNINE CULT

Ying Chao

FROM THE OPENING LECTURE IN A NEW MOOC (MASSIVE OPEN ONLINE COURSE) CALLED "CRITICAL CONSPIRACIES". THE COURSE WAS CANCELLED FOLLOWING THE RESIGNATION OF THE INSTRUCTOR, MS. YING CHAO. NOTES SUBMITTED TO MARTINET PRESS FOR DISTRIBUTION.

[TAKE ATTENDANCE. CREDIT WIKIMEDIA FOR SLIDES]

Good morning, and welcome to the opening lecture of 'Critical Conspiracies', a Massive Open Online Course focusing on critical analysis of modern conspiracy theories. I'm Ying Chao, and I'll be your instructor for the next six weeks. We begin today with an examination of the world's most insidious cult, which, if real, affects all of us daily, hides in plain sight, and engages in warfare and subversion on a scale complete undreamed of by most critical theorists.

Many conspiracy theorists today express a great deal of interest in secret societies, conspiracies, the supernatural, and religious sects. For this reason, the "satanic" sects of the occult have often been a favorite topic for conspiracy theorists. For example, some satanic societies claim that they are in contact with astral or spiritual "masters," and that they have had experiences to validate their beliefs in these "masters." This may in fact be the case. In fact, it is reasonable to hypothesize that there may actually be multiple supernatural intelligences, which can and do interact with esoteric societies, and that these entities can cause manifestations, communications, and abnormal phenomena. This hypothesis does not, of course, imply that we accepts the claims of whatever entities a society might commune with – it simply means that we could accept that a satanic group could be communicating some inhuman force or intelligence. Whether or not their theology or communiqués are "truth" can only be discussed on a case-by-case basis. By the same logic, one must admit that Hindus, Catholics, and Buddhists *do* experience abnormal phenomena –

this has been documented – but that does *not* mean that one has to accept the entire theology of a sect in order to accept that they have experienced any particular phenomena.

In any event, this lecture is not about the visible satanic sects of today. Instead, the goal of this lecture is to introduce you to the original "black" cult, that secret society which really does operate behind the scenes, and is genuinely engineering social and political change. You can believe this or not, but the evidence speaks for itself.

This opening lecture on "Critical Conspiracies" is intended to reveal the hidden Cult of Saturn, the original dark lord, who is also called Cronos, Zuhal, Moloch, Śanaiścara, Baal, Azazel, and Samedi.

THE TWENTIETH CENTURY

In the last twenty years, one of the greatest advances in the western "satanic" community has been the diversification of traditions and practices, which have been co-opted and adapted for sinister purposes. So, Crowley is sometimes named as the original inspiration for the later "Satanic" movements of the 20th century. Despite his brilliance, however, Crowley's legacy has been a very confused state of affairs, with Anton LaVey having tried to dismiss Crowley, and Michael Aquino having tried to emulate Crowley, yet neither succeeding especially well at stepping out of his shadow. The Order of the Golden Dawn and its affiliates fared no better, as they struggled with the confusing doctrine of *thelema*, and lacked Crowley's erudition and creativity. This lead eventually to a general degradation of the occult field. On a similar note, with the death or retirement of their founders, the Church of Satan and Temple of Set have both fallen considerably from their places of prominence in the 1970s and 1980s, and have experienced their own internal issues of leadership or financial hardship.

That said, we should note that in the late 1970s, there appeared an independent esoteric pioneer writing under the name "Anton Long", who's Order of Nine Angles demonstrated a fresh and original take on the hermetic current. Long's work drew inspiration from Arthurian and Hermetic practices, and clearly showed that one's native locale can serve as an important source of esoteric knowledge. The ONA in turn inspired other esoteric lodges. Some of these gracefully acknowledged the debt to the Order, where others more tacitly borrowed Long's thinking and freely adapted his vocabulary and mythos – which appears to be in line with his ambitions all along. The ONA has enjoyed a wide notoriety among conspiracy theorists, as it has a strong activist character in addition to its esoteric doctrines.

SINCE 2000

Since 2000, a new wave of esoteric publishers and currents has appeared, and most of these are generally dividable along three "streams". The first stream is the **New Qlippoth** movement, the second stream is the **Afro-Caribbean** movement, and the third is the ever-popular **Chaos-Gnostic** movement. These are my own terms, and you can alternate your own names for these very broad movements, if you find it easier.

The first of these (**New Qlippoth**) movements to involve an inverted study of the Jewish kabbalah, adapted liberally from the works of Nathan of Gaza and related Jewish mystics. The concept of the *qlippoth* (Heb. shell) is used as a sort of antithesis to the traditional Jewish model. Lilith and Satan are evident in these traditions, which appear to be a kind of "Satanic" Judaism, which parallels the genuine (Catholic) Satanism of the mediaeval period. The second group

(**Afro-Caribbean**) may have taken inspiration from the *Voudou* work of Michael Bertiaux, but in the last decade, this field has grown to include devotees of more Hispanic-influenced traditions like Candomblé and Quimbanda. Devotees of these rites tend to focus on the Satan-analogues in these traditions, and some very interesting work has begun to appear in the public domain. The third group (**Chaos Gnostics**) are themselves may be a development of the resurgence of Gnostic Christianity in the 1950s, but instead of worshiping the Demiurge or the Devil, they focus on ancient concepts of the Original Chaos, or Abyss, which takes the place of the usual Gnostic deity. Union with the Original Chaos is sought, and Satan (Lilith, Samael, etc) may be intermediaries in this quest.

At this point, you might be thinking to yourself: don't some modern occult groups technically fit into all three categories above? The answer can only be that some groups are definitely *trying* to be all three, and some are more successful than others. One must concede that there is nothing necessarily wrong with syncretism, which is a hallmark of the world's other mainstream religious movements.

But, as stated in the introduction, this lecture focuses on the Hidden Cult of Saturn, and its public and private manifestations.

The study of comparative mythology is often revealing and useful to the modern student of conspiracy. When someone studies the ancient myths and legends carefully, they will discover that there is a strange and terrible god, known by all, feared by many, worshipped by some, and loved by few. The Hidden Cult teaches that He rules all in secret from a cold and distant place. They say that His hand stretches towards us, bending all Fates to His terrible will. The claim that He has many titles: the night-thunder, the reaper, the lord of time, the first of all things. He is the all-father, and the devourer of children. He is the brazen bull, and lord of the Black Stone. This god the Romans called Saturn, the Greeks named him Cronos, in Carthage he was Moloch, in India Shanaishchara, while the Jews and Moslems named him Zohal.

ON SATURN IN ANCIENT TIMES

The Romans called him Saturn ("grim, gloomy"), and they named Him first among the titans. They worshipped him with grain, oil, and wine; but also with blood, sacrificing black bulls and criminals to him in the gladiatorial games. His colors were black and blue, and his nature was said to be "cold and dry". They feared him so greatly that His idol was veiled, and the legs were bound as though a captive. In December, however, they unchained His legs, and celebrated the Feast of Saturnalia – a wild and debauched festival when slaves and masters changed places, and chaos ruled. The public treasury was kept at his temple, and it is said that Rome itself was called Mons Saturnia (Mount Saturn) in the ancient times. While Jupiter replaced Him as the chief of the gods, the Romans believed that Saturn would someday return to power, and overthrow the corrupt and selfish gods of the republic. Saturn was the ultimate tyrant, and ruled over humanity by establishing divine governors to rule all human affairs. The Romans believed that the day would come when Saturn again seized control of the world, ushering in a glorious new era. Saturn's reign is referred to as *Saturnia Regna*, which the Romans understood to be a totalitarian utopia, where Saturn would reign as the ultimate despot. It would be an enlightened tyranny, where justice is true because it is divorced from the corrupting hands of mortals. Saturn, for the Romans, was an extremely complex figure: he was an agricultural god, but only of reaping and harvest. Pluto was considered the god of the dead, but Saturn is the god of necromancy, especially in later times. Where Pluto and Jupiter enforced cosmic order, Saturn overturned it at will, for which reason He was feared and his statue was bound.

TEMPLE OF SATURN, ROMA

This said, the Romans believed that Saturn's return to power was inevitable. In the *Eclogues* of Virgil, it is written:

Ultima Cumaei venit iam carminis aetas;
Magnus ab integro saeclorum nascitur ordo.
iam redit et Virgo, **redeunt Saturnia regna**,

iam nova progenies caelo demittitur alto.

Now comes the final era of the Sibyl's song;
The new world order is born.
And now justice returns, **Saturn's reign restored**;

Now a new lineage is sent down from high heaven.

Strange, is it not, that from this same verse comes the American phrase: *Novus ordo seclorum...*?

[*PAUSE FOR EFFECT. TAKE QUESTIONS.*]

GOD OF TIME

The Greeks too believed in this grim god, calling him Cronus ("The Cutter") or Xronos ("Time"), and like the Romans, they believed that He was the First King, father of gods and humans. Cronus is a chthonic god for the Greeks, as He is exiled by Zeus after the war of the gods and titans. While Saturn was worshipped (if dreaded) by the Romans, the Greeks feared and hated Cronus for his legendary cruelty. The Greeks taught that He devoured the other gods, hating them for their rebellion and free will. While Zeus and his siblings managed to overcome Cronus, they were unable to kill him, and assigned him to rule the underworld kingdom of Tartarus. Cronus then becomes a figure of importance for the Greek and Hellenistic magicians, who called upon him in their magical incantations. The *Greek Magical Papyri* (e.g. PGM IV. 3086-3124) has several spells that call on Cronos as the Master of Time and Fate, and He was worshipped as an oracular deity. Aside from the Cronia festival, there was no organized cult of Cronus, apart from witches and magicians who prayed to this chthonic god to help alter the Fates. Like the Romans, the Greeks believed that Cronus was best propitiated with black color and black, bitter sacrifices, such as black olives or black wines, in addition to salt.

DEVOURER OF GODS AND MEN

The North Africans celebrated the cult of Saturn under the name "Baal Hamon", also called "Moloch" or "Saturnus Africanus". Records indicate that this cult practiced rituals of propitiation, offering blood sacrifices to the deity in order to celebrate a good harvest, and to ward off their enemies. The African cult was famous for its human sacrifices, which were burned alive according to Greek and Roman tradition. There is relatively little records on the cult of Moloch, and what we know comes largely from Christian sources who were trying to vilify the cult. The few images of Saturn

Africanus depict him in the Roman style, veiled and somber.

SATURN IN MEDIEVAL EUROPE

[show slide]

> Later medieval books of magic are seldom shy about giving straightforwardly harmful formulas. A fifteenth-century *Liber de angelis, annulis, karecteribus et ymaginibus planetarum (Book of angels, rings, characters, and images of the planets)* in the Cambridge University Library contains an experiment called the *Vindicta Troie (Vengeance of Troy)*, which can be used to arouse hatred or to cause bodily harm or even death. The procedure calls for making an image on the day and in the hour of Saturn, in the name of the person to be harmed. The image must be made of wax, preferably from candles used at a funeral. It should be made as ugly as possible; the face should be contorted, and there should be hands in place of feet and vice versa. The victim's name should be inscribed on the forehead of the image, the name of the planet Saturn on its breast, and the seals or characters of Saturn between its shoulders. The operator should call upon the spirits of Saturn to descend from on high and afflict the named victim. The image should be fumigated with various substances, including human bones and hair, then wrapped in a funeral cloth and buried in some unclean place, face downward. If the magician wishes to harm any particular member of the victim's body, there are instructions for binding the corresponding member on the image with a funeral cloth and piercing the image with a needle; to kill the victim, the magician should insert the needle into the spine, from the head down to the

This is a single example from a wide range of occult manuscripts, which indicate that Saturn continued to be propitiated as a spiritual force of malice and harm. Saturday is considered to be the day sacred to Saturn, and his chthonic, funeral character is still very intact.

GOD OF THE BLACK STONE

Like the Greeks and Romans, the Jews and Moslems have always worshipped Saturn (Zohal). "Zohal" means "the one who is far away", and He was believed to inhabit the most distant reaches of the cosmos. Zohal is a dark and gloomy spirit, not really of this world, but not totally alien to it either. The Jewish Sabbath is on Saturday, which is why the Jews felt a special affinity for this particular pagan god.

The medieval Arab writing Al Majiriti wrote of Him:

"Address yourself to Saturn for requests made to the elderly, generous people, the leaders of cities, kings, hermits, men who work the earth, the functionaries of cities and properties, remarkable people, farmers, slaves, thieves, fathers, the ancestors and ancient ancestors. If you have dark thoughts and suffer, afflicted by melancholy or weakness, for all that follows or comes before, address yourself to Saturn regarding whatever is of His nature. When you address Saturn, dress yourself in black. Betake yourself to the proper place on Saturday, having in hand an iron ring, and take with you a censor in which you place charcoal burning with incense. Having censed the place, speak thus:

> 'Oh great master who possesses a great name and who is situated above all planets, you [who are placed] high and in an elevated place. You are the Lord Saturn, cold and dry, shadowy, author of good, true in

Your friendship, sincere in Your promises, persistent and tenacious in Your in your friendships and enmities, of tenacious and profound intellect, true in Your sayings and Your promises, unique in Your operations, separate from the other gods, with sorrow and suffering, distant from mindless pleasure. You are old one, the ancient, at once wise and a destroyer of good judgement, you mix good and evil. Sad and unhappy is he who vexes You, happy is he whom You favor. In you are placed virtue and power, a spirit of doing good and evil. I demand, father and lord, by Your high names and Your marvelous actions to do for me such and such.... I call You by Your names, you in the seventh heaven: Zohal (Arabic), Saturn (Latin), Keyvan (Persian), Chronos (Greek), Sacas (Sanskrit).'

Now state your request, confident that it shall be accomplished."

The Moslems used this as his sigil:

[*PAUSE FOR EFFECT. TAKE QUESTIONS.*]

It is important to note that Sabian sorcerer, Ibn Wahshiyya, writes on Saturn in his famous occult treatise:

"One should this prayer to Saturn and ask him for what one wants, addressing the prayer to his image, in order to get the response that one wants. You should worship him in the image of a black stone, which is His idol. Here is how the prayer goes:

'Worship and prayer, we address to you, standing, we ask and we honor you with obedience and humility. We address you, standing and facing the exalted master, the Alive, the Eternal, eternal, solid in his power and dominion, you are Saturn. You are eternal in his heaven and mighty in his dominion, focuses in his efforts and his great works. You are over all, his power is over all living things on earth, and they endure by His endurance. By Your power and Your might You began them, and You make them to continue; he causes us to endure, and by Your eternity and perpetuity, You brings permanence on earth. By Your might, You cause the waters to ebb and flow.

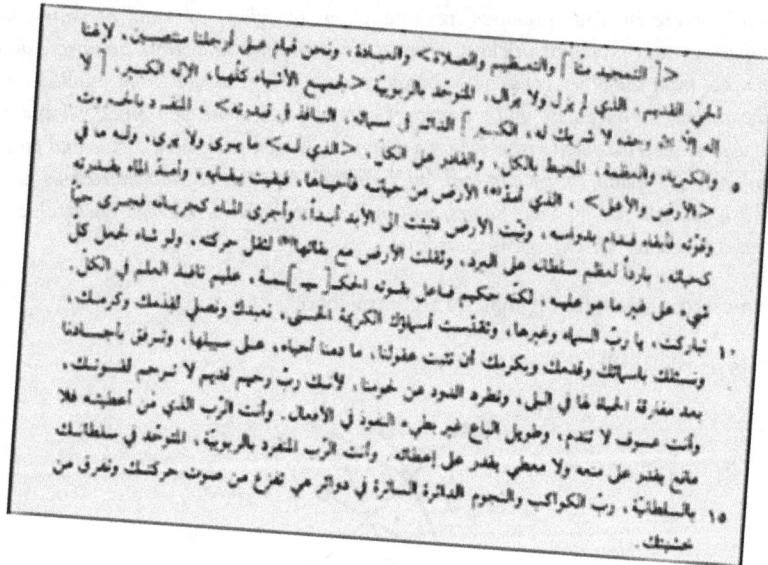

Living, You cause life to move, because You are Alive. You are cold, as is Your nature. Through the influence of Your high realm, the trees grow, and the earth becomes heavy under the weight of Your movements; if You wishes, You cause beings to become what they are not. Yet You are wise and a creator by Your might and intelligence; Your Knowledge extends to all things. Hail, lord of the heavens, may Your name be holy, pure and honored. We obey you; we address ourselves to Your feet, we call you by your names, your heart, your nobility and honor, we request from You whom we respect to strengthen our mind, that it be strong and enduring and dwell in us while we live. Then when we die, ward off the worms and reptiles from our flesh. You are the merciful and ancient Teacher, and no one can save the one you condemn. You are persistent in your words and deeds, and you regret not your acts. You are slow and profound in your powers. You are a master whose deeds cannot be undone, and what you forbid cannot be done by another. You are respected in all your actions and unique in your kingdom. You are the lord of the other planets, and the very stars fear the sound of your movement and tremble before your gaze. We ask ask and demand you to avert Your dark influence from us, and in your purity, to treat us well. By Your good and noble names, we avert Your sinister qualities, and we draw from your virtue. By your names, by your True Name which you love more than the others, treat us well and grant what we ask.'"

But what is the 'Black Stone' of Zohal? The answer is in Mecca, of course.

[*PAUSE FOR LAUGHTER. DELAY QUESTIONS.*]

In other words, Islam is one of the great modern cults of Saturn. Perhaps given that Saturn is a violent and cruel deity, we can understand to some extent why Islam remains a problematic religion, dedicated to oppression in its most obvious forms. The various wars and conflicts are part of the mass sacrifices needed to appease the chthonic deity. And the image of the black cube is everywhere today. Modern art, films, media, car companies.

It is important to note that the famous Moslem heretics, the so-called "Brethren of Purity", taught their founder, Shaykh Idriss (Hermes Trismegistos), had passed through a star-gate and ascended to the celestial orbit of Saturn, and had spent thirty years there learning the secrets of the cosmos. After this, he descended to earth, and taught the Hermetic corpus. So, Saturn is the secret master behind of the Seven Fold Way.

It is clearly no coincidence that years later, the British mystic Anton Long would uncover the writings consistent with the Hermetic teachings of the Brethren of Purity, and propagate his own secret doctrine that a "star gate" is near Saturn, and one must pass through the various planets to eventually reach the Saturnian sphere of understanding and personal transformation.

LORD OF THE DEAD

In the Afro-Carribean religions , Saturn is worshipped today as *Baron Samedi*, a chthonic loa (deity) who leads the spirits of the dead. While he maintains his sardonic character, he is known for his dark sense of humor. Samedi (French for "Saturn" or "Saturday") dresses in expensive (if tattered) clothing, and his offerings involve tobacco and rum. Baron Samedi is connected with the modern idea of the zombie, as well as being the patron of necromancy and black magic. One turns to Baron Samedi for magical requests which are too sinister or vile to be address to the more mainstream or benevolent loa. While Baron Samedi isn't evil (in the sense that Satan is evil), he is malevolent – he likes to harm and cause harm, or else a very black mischief.

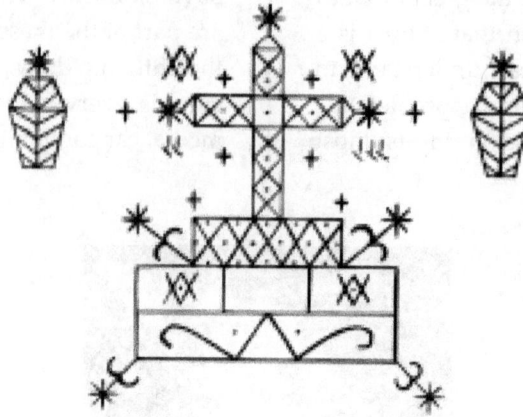

THE VÉVÉ OF BARON SAMEDI

The Haitian leader Papa Doc Duvalier modelled his own persona on the character of Samedi, and was publically acknowleged as a devotee of this sinister entity. Saturn in this guise maintains a popular cult today in Haiti and the African diaspora regions. Baron Samedi dresses in black, and is sometimes depicted with a walking stick, indicating that he is lame or sluggish of step.

LORD OF KARMA

Hinduism venerates Saturn as Lord Śanaiścara, the son of Surya (the solar deity). As with the other cultures noted earlier in this lecture, Saturn/Śanaiścara is considered to be the lord of Saturday, and is depicted dressed in black and blue clothing. He is the lord of the planet Saturn, and Hindus revere him with offerings on Saturdays, usually of sugar and grain, which can be given to crows, ravens, black animals, and to socially dispossessed people. He is described as lame or injured in some way.

Lord Śanaiścara is not a popular deity in India, but his cult is still very active. His idols are curiously sometimes merely black obelisks (stones), and like his Western counterparts, he is called on to avert harm, or to fulfill forbidden desires that people cannot take to more popular (or respectable) deities. Saturn is propitiated through the Sanskrit mantra *Om Sham Shri Śanaiścaraya Namaha.*

SUMMARY REMARKS

This lecture concludes with the following observations. The cult of Saturn is *cross-cultural* and *international*. The various incarnations of Saturn share very similar features.

- The colors black and blue are sacred to him
- The crow, the raven, and black bulls are especially sacred to him.
- He is both a chthonic/infernal deity, with control over fate/time/karma
- He is an outcast god who seeks to return to the center.
- His worship involves blood sacrifices and criminal intentions.
- He is a god of secrets and intrigue.
- He is often lame, or slow, or chained.
- He is entirely amoral and frequently associated with requests that are too profane for other gods.

If the Hidden Cult of Saturn is real, it is the most successful cult in the world. American and Muslim politics are part of its operating strategy, and it acts with impunity in arranging conflict and hostility. If someone wished to join this cult, then there are multiple points of entry: the Hermetic systems, the Voudou cults, and the Hindu cult of Saturn are several which survive today. Whether or not one accepts that Saturn is a real intelligence or deity, the Saturnine conspiracy itself is very real, and very well documented, when one accepts the data at face value.

Thanks for your attention, I hope you enjoyed the lecture. See you next class.

Sarah Wreck
Shitty Occult Comics